Congressional
Research
Service

The Interplay of Borders, Turf, Cyberspace, and Jurisdiction: Issues Confronting U.S. Law Enforcement

Kristin M. Finklea
Specialist in Domestic Security

July 20, 2012

Congressional Research Service

7-5700

www.crs.gov

R41927

CRS Report for Congress
Prepared for Members and Committees of Congress

Summary

Savvy criminals constantly develop new techniques to target U.S. persons, businesses, and interests. Individual criminals as well as broad criminal networks exploit geographic borders, criminal turf, cyberspace, and law enforcement jurisdiction to dodge law enforcement countermeasures. Further, the interplay of these realities can potentially encumber policing measures. In light of these interwoven realities, policy makers may question how to best design policies to help law enforcement combat ever-evolving criminal threats.

Criminals routinely take advantage of geographic borders. They thrive on their ability to illicitly cross borders, subvert border security regimens, and provide illegal products or services. Many crimes—particularly those of a cyber nature—have become increasingly transnational. While criminals may operate across geographic borders and jurisdictional boundaries, law enforcement may not be able to do so with the same ease. Moreover, obstacles such as disparities between the legal regimens of nations (what is considered a crime in one country may not be in another) and differences in willingness to extradite suspected criminals can hamper prosecutions. The law enforcement community has, however, expanded its working relationships with both domestic and international agencies.

Globalization and technological innovation have fostered the expansion of both legitimate and criminal operations across physical borders as well as throughout cyberspace. Advanced, rapid communication systems have made it easier for criminals to carry out their operations remotely from their victims and members of their illicit networks. In the largely borderless cyber domain, criminals can rely on relative anonymity and a rather seamless environment to conduct illicit business. Further, in the rapidly evolving digital age, law enforcement may not have the technological capabilities to keep up with the pace of criminals.

Some criminal groups establish their own operational "borders" by defining and defending the "turf" or territories they control. Similarly, U.S. law enforcement often remains constrained by its own notions of "turf"—partly defined in terms of competing agency-level priorities and jurisdictions. While some crimes are worked under the jurisdiction of a proprietary agency, others are not investigated under such clear lines. These investigative overlaps and a lack of data and information sharing can hinder law enforcement anti-crime efforts.

U.S. law enforcement has, particularly since the terrorist attacks of September 11, 2001, increasingly relied on intelligence-led policing, enhanced interagency cooperation, and technological implementation to confront 21st century crime. For instance, enforcement agencies have used formal and informal interagency agreements as well as fusion centers and task forces to assimilate information and coordinate operations. Nonetheless, there have been notable impediments in implementing effective information sharing systems and relying on up-to-date technology. Congress may question how it can leverage its legislative and oversight roles to bolster U.S. law enforcement's abilities to confront modern-day crime. For instance, Congress may consider whether federal law enforcement has the existing authorities, technology, and resources—both monetary and manpower—to counter 21st century criminals (particularly cybercriminals, e.g., S. 2105, S. 3414). Congress may also examine whether federal law enforcement is utilizing existing mechanisms to effectively coordinate investigations and share information.

Contents

Figures

Contacts

Introduction

Savvy criminals constantly develop new techniques to target U.S. persons, businesses, and interests. Central to the evolution of modern-day crime are four broad operational realities—geographic borders, criminal turf, cyberspace, and law enforcement jurisdiction. Individual criminals as well as broad criminal networks exploit these realities and often leverage the unique characteristics of one against the other to dodge law enforcement countermeasures and efforts to disrupt illicit activity. Further, the *interplay* of these realities can potentially encumber policing measures. In light of these interwoven realities, policy makers may question how to best design policies to help law enforcement combat ever-evolving criminal threats.

In the first operational reality, criminals routinely take advantage of geographic lines. They thrive on their ability to illicitly cross borders and provide illegal products or services. Indeed, much criminal activity is predicated on the ability to subvert border security regimens, thus earning a premium from black market clients and customers. Drug trafficking organizations (DTOs), for example, have constructed increasingly sophisticated cross-border tunnels to smuggle illegal drugs from Mexico into the United States. And, smugglers and fraudsters ship counterfeit goods from overseas, flooding U.S. markets with sham goods and depriving genuine manufacturers of profits.

The second reality is broadly related to the first. Some larger criminal groups even establish their own operational "borders" by defining and defending the "turf" or territories they control. These boundaries are not formally recognized by law enforcement authorities, but they have strong influence in the criminal underworld. In fact, much of the violence in Mexico along the U.S. Southwest border revolves around rival DTOs clashing over territorial control.[1] The outlines of turf can cross borders at the national, state, and local levels, thus complicating policing efforts.

The third reality involves a largely borderless, virtual environment where criminals carry out illicit business. Criminals operate in the cyber world partly to circumvent more conventional, established constructs such as international borders. In the virtual realm, criminals can rely on relative anonymity and a rather seamless environment to conduct business. For instance, some criminals use electronic banking systems to quickly smuggle cash out of one nation and into another.

Finally, U.S. law enforcement often remains constrained by geographic and legal boundaries or even its own notions of "turf"—partly defined in terms of competing agency-level priorities and jurisdictions. U.S. officials have suggested that as criminals have evolved their operations, they have relied less on turf to conduct business;[2] the same evolution is unclear regarding U.S. law enforcement. Law enforcement agencies, even while collaborating through means such as interagency agreements, task forces, and fusion centers, retain investigational jurisdiction over

---

[1] For more information on the drug trafficking-related violence in Mexico, see CRS Report R41576, *Mexico's Drug Trafficking Organizations: Source and Scope of the Rising Violence*, by June S. Beittel.

[2] U.S. Department of Justice, *FY2012 Performance Budget, Drug Enforcement Administration, U.S. Department of Justice, Congressional Budget Submission*, p. 11, http://www.justice.gov/jmd/2012justification/pdf/fy12-dea-justification.pdf.

certain categories of crime. And recent reports have suggested that interagency disagreements over organizational boundaries may remain.[3]

In addition to challenges presented by each of these four operational realities individually, law enforcement faces hurdles presented by the overlap of any or all of the realities. Complicating this, policy changes in one reality—both administratively and legislatively—can impact criminal activity and law enforcement countermeasures in other realities. Policy makers have expressed interest in ensuring that law enforcement is keeping pace with 21st century criminals who threaten American society.[4]

Given that criminal investigations unfold in an environment of geographic borders, criminal turf, borderless cyberspace, and law enforcement jurisdictions, policy makers may question how to direct policy to best enable U.S. law enforcement to target contemporary criminals. For instance, Congress may choose to examine whether law enforcement agencies are effectively coordinating their investigations through the use of interagency agreements, task forces, and fusion centers. Policy makers may also debate whether law enforcement has the existing legal authorities, technology, and resources—both financial and manpower—to counter 21st century criminals. One of the principal debates for policy makers may be whether, or how, to design policies that cut across multiple operational realities.

This report examines the four operational realities within which law enforcement and crime operate. It analyzes the challenges for U.S. law enforcement in each of these realities individually and in selected cases where they overlap. The report also discusses how law enforcement has adapted to combat present-day criminals. Throughout, it raises questions regarding how Congress may leverage its legislative and oversight roles to help U.S. law enforcement most effectively protect U.S. persons, businesses, and interests.

Boundaries in the Operational Realities

Physical and virtual boundaries play significant roles in both criminal activity and police work. In the physical world, recognized borders delineate the lines of municipal, state, and national authority. At their most basic level, legally defined geographic borders outline the sovereignty of these entities. For example, at official crossings along the U.S. border with Mexico, law enforcement presence helps to distinguish one nation from another. Between ports of entry, the U.S. Customs and Border Protection (CBP) has deployed personnel, technology, and tactical infrastructure along the Southwest border to impede the illegal entry of vehicles and unauthorized persons. When it comes to criminal turf, the virtual realm, and law enforcement jurisdictions, the lines separating one authority—legitimate or illegitimate—from another often grow fuzzier. The following sections lay out discussions of borders, turf, cyberspace (the virtual world), and jurisdiction that help shape modern criminal activity as well as law enforcement counter efforts.

---

[3] U.S. Government Accountability Office, *Law Enforcement Coordination: DOJ Could Improve Its Process for Identifying Disagreements Among Agents*, GAO-11-314, April 2011, p. 2, http://www.gao.gov/new.items/d11314.pdf. See also U.S. Department of Justice, Office of the Inspector General, Audit Division, *The Federal Bureau of Investigation's Ability to Address the National Security Cyber Intrusion Threat*, Audit Report 11-22, April 2011, pp. iv - vii, http://www.justice.gov/oig/reports/FBI/a1122r.pdf.

[4] See U.S. Congress, Senate Committee on the Judiciary, Subcommittee on Crime and Terrorism, *Cybersecurity: Responding to the Threat of Cyber Crime and Terrorism*, 112th Cong., 1st sess., April 12, 2011.

Borders

As suggested, physical or geographic borders—whether they divide countries, states, or even neighbors' plots of land—are often recognized with relative ease. Frequently, there are signals indicating when one is entering or leaving a given geographic area. Road signs, for instance, may provide notice of crossing from one city, county, state, etc., to another. International border checkpoints can signal that one is entering or leaving a country. Along several portions of the Southwest border, a fence separates the United States from Mexico.[5] Such physical boundaries may aid in delineating the space within which a given set of rules applies.[6]

Nations have sovereign control over their countries and territories and may enforce the laws of their lands within those bounds. In the United States, the federal government is responsible for enforcing federal laws within the country, and each state is responsible for enforcing state laws within its physical borders. And, rules that hold in one state may not apply in a neighboring state with different laws. For example, stealing $400 worth of goods is considered felony theft in California, but a criminal needs to steal $1,000 worth of goods in neighboring Arizona for the crime to reach the felony theft threshold.[7] Similarly, laws that apply in certain states may not apply under federal law to the country as a whole.

Globalization, technological innovation, and heightened security concerns have complicated traditional understanding of borders. Business, for instance, has become increasingly borderless;[8] so, too, have criminal enterprises. Since the terrorist attacks of September 11, 2001, the United States has experienced an expanded tension between border protection concerns and free market ideals.[9] Open border regimens are encouraged by a desire for efficiently moving goods and services. However, security screenings and concerns over safety may slow down the transit of these items. Criminals may then capitalize on any weaknesses in border regimens to supply black market goods and services where there is a demand. In other words, border protection systems and enforcement efforts can have the unintended consequence of introducing inefficiencies to market systems. These inefficiencies can, in turn, present profitable opportunities for criminal networks.[10]

Turf

Some criminals—such as drug cartels and street gangs—have established turf boundaries for their operations. These boundaries may or may not coincide with geographically and legally defined borders. Criminal turf often delineates a territory within which illegal entities carry out their operations. In the United States, street gang warfare has historically centered around the

---

[5] For more information, see archived CRS Report RL33659, *Border Security: Barriers Along the U.S. International Border*, by Chad C. Haddal and Michael John Garcia.

[6] David R. Johnson and David Post, "Law and Borders—The Rise of Law in Cyberspace," *Stanford Law Review*, vol. 48 (May 1996), p. 1370.

[7] See the Appendix of CRS Report R41118, *Organized Retail Crime*, by Kristin M. Finklea.

[8] National Intelligence Council, *Global Trends 2025: A Transformed World*, NIC 2008-003, November 2008, p. 17, http://www.dni.gov/nic/PDF_2025/2025_Global_Trends_Final_Report.pdf.

[9] CRS Report R41237, *People Crossing Borders: An Analysis of U.S. Border Protection Policies*, by Alison Siskin.

[10] Ibid.

---

establishment and protection of turf.[11] Other criminal networks have used various means to establish operational turf as well.

For instance, in February 2011, 22 members of a violent, fraudulent document-trafficking organization (including the manager of the organization's U.S. operations) were indicted for crimes including the use of "brutal violence to eliminate rivals, protect its turf and enforce discipline against its own members."[12] The organization, based in Mexico, has operations in 19 U.S. cities and 11 states, selling counterfeit Resident Alien and Social Security cards to unauthorized immigrants. The suspects in this case allegedly protected the organization's turf by posing as customers looking to buy the counterfeit identification cards. The "customers" would then attack competitors when they met for a supposed sale. Victims' hands, feet, and mouths were bound, and they were beaten and threatened with death should they continue to operate on the organization's turf.[13]

Turf may be readily established in the real world, as criminals can rely upon the physical environment to establish territory. In the cyber world, however, it may appear to be difficult to establish virtual turf lines, but they exist nonetheless. For example, two Trojans,[14] believed to be based in Russia, engaged in a cyber turf battle in 2010. The two Trojans—ZeuS and its smaller competitor, SpyEye—would both steal online banking information. They would then transfer funds to money mules, or U.S. residents with bank accounts, who would then move the money out of the United States. SpyEye challenged ZeuS by stealing information from ZeuS and then removing the ZeuS toolkit from infected computers.[15] The turf war reportedly ended when the ZeuS Trojan was no longer maintained and its code was allegedly merged with that of SpyEye.[16]

Cyberspace

As mentioned, the relatively clear borders and turf lines within the physical world are not replicated in the virtual realm. Of course, some distinct boundaries separate the physical and the cyber worlds; a keyboard, mouse, screen, and password can all mediate between these physical and virtual realms.[17] Within cyberspace, however, the notion of a border is much more nebulous.

---

[11] James C. Howell and John P. Moore, *History of Street Gangs in the United States*, U.S. Department of Justice, Bureau of Justice Assistance, Office of Juvenile Justice and Delinquency Prevention, May 2010, http://www.ojp.usdoj.gov/BJA/pdf/NGC_History_Street_Gangs.pdf.

[12] Statement of U.S. Attorney MacBride, United States Attorneys Office, "Twenty-Two Alleged Members of Sophisticated, Violent Fraudulent Document Ring Indicted," press release, February 24, 2011, http://www.justice.gov/usao/vae/news/2011/02/20110224arellanonr.html.

[13] Ibid.

[14] A Trojan is a type of malware. It is a type of software that, once activated, can damage the host and provide back doors for malicious users to access the computer system. For more information on the various types of malware, see Cisco, *What Is the Difference: Viruses, Worms, Trojans, and Bots?*, http://www.cisco.com/web/about/security/intelligence/virus-worm-diffs.html.

[15] "SpyEye vs. ZeuS Rivalry," *krebsonsecurity.com*, April 1, 2010, http://krebsonsecurity.com/2010/04/spyeye-vs-zeus-rivalry/. See also Nick Farrell, "Cyber gangs fight turf war, From Russia with Love," *TechEye.net*, February 10, 2011, http://www.techeye.net/security/cyber-gangs-fight-turf-war.

[16] "SpyEye vs. ZeuS Rivalry Ends in Quiet Merger," *krebsonsecurity.com*, October 24, 2010, http://krebsonsecurity.com/2010/10/spyeye-v-zeus-rivalry-ends-in-quiet-merger/.

[17] David R. Johnson and David Post, "Law and Borders—The Rise of Law in Cyberspace," *Stanford Law Review*, vol. 48 (May 1996), p. 1379.

This is, in part, because the same geographic borders that exist in the real world do not exist in the cyber world.[18]

High-speed internet communication has not only facilitated the growth of legitimate business, but it has bolstered criminals' abilities to operate in an environment where they can broaden their pool of potential targets and rapidly exploit their victims. Between 2000 and 2010, the estimated number of internet users grew from almost 361 million to nearly 2 billion—an increase of more than 444%.[19] Frauds and schemes that were once conducted face-to-face can now be carried out remotely from across the country or even across the world. The United Nations Office on Drugs and Crime notes that cybercrime has "evolved from the mischievous one-upmanship of cyber-vandals to a range of profit-making criminal enterprises in a remarkably short time."[20] U.S. policy makers, officials, and law enforcement have become increasingly concerned about the threats posed by criminals in the virtual world.[21]

Even cyberspace, though, has some boundaries—both technological and jurisdictional. Some web addresses, for instance, are country-specific, and the administration of those websites is controlled by particular nations. For instance, website addresses ending in ".us" indicate that the United States owns the server controlling the website, while those ending in ".au" indicate Australian control.[22] Another barrier in cyberspace may involve subscriptions or fee-based access to particular website content. Certain businesses—news sites, journals, file sharing sites, and others—may require paid access. There are also legal parameters governing what private citizens or law enforcement can lawfully do online. Despite this, an enhanced sense of anonymity offered to actors in the cyber world may encourage illicit behavior.

Certain traditional crimes such as fraud and identity theft are increasingly being seen as typical cybercrimes. A primary difference between these lines in the cyber and physical worlds is the venue in which crimes are committed. It appears that many crimes considered cybercrimes could be considered traditional, or "real world," crimes if not for the virtual venue in which they occur. On one hand, the virtual world may be seen as a borderless *space* that provides criminals with relative anonymity and a place to operate. However, cyberspace can also be seen as a *tool* that criminals use to subvert borders. Due to the global nature of the internet and other rapid communication systems, crimes committed via or with the aid of the internet can quickly impact victims in multiple state and national jurisdictions.

---

[18] David R. Johnson and David Post, "Law and Borders—The Rise of Law in Cyberspace," *Stanford Law Review*, vol. 48 (May 1996), p. 1370.

[19] Internet World Stats, *Internet Usage Statistics, The Internet Big Picture, World Internet Users and Population Stats*, http://www.internetworldstats.com/stats.htm.

[20] United Nations Office on Drugs and Crime, *The Globalization of Crime: A Transnational Organized Crime Threat Assessment*, ISBN: 978-92-1-130295-0, 2010, p. 203, http://www.unodc.org/documents/data-and-analysis/tocta/TOCTA_Report_2010_low_res.pdf.

[21] The 112th Congress has held several hearings on such threats. See, for example, U.S. Congress, House Committee on the Judiciary, Subcommittee on Intellectual Property, Competition and the Internet, *Cybersecurity: Innovative Solutions to Challenging Problems*, 112th Cong., 1st sess., May 25, 2011; and U.S. Congress, House Committee on the Judiciary, Subcommittee on Crime, Terrorism, and Homeland Security, *Data Retention as a Tool for Investigating Internet Child Pornography and Other Internet Crimes*, 112th Cong., 1st sess., January 25, 2011.

[22] The Internet Assigned Numbers Authority (IANA) is responsible for managing internet domain names, the Internet Protocol addressing systems, and the Autonomous System Numbers used for routing internet traffic. See http://www.iana.org/. See also CRS Report 97-868, *Internet Domain Names: Background and Policy Issues*, by Lennard G. Kruger.

Recent congressional testimony from a Department of Justice (DOJ) official indicated that most cybersecurity incidents are transnational in nature.[23] For instance, in May 2010, U.S. law enforcement indicted three individuals, located in the United States, Ukraine, and Sweden, for their roles in an international scareware scam.[24] The alleged fraudsters led internet users in these countries to falsely believe that their computers had become infected with malware. They then enticed their victims into buying bogus scareware software products that they advertised would remedy the contaminated computers. In reality, the software had no effect, as the supposedly infected computers were not truly compromised. This scam resulted in over $100 million in total losses.

Transnational cases such as this may raise proprietary questions regarding case investigation and prosecution and may cause significant challenges for law enforcement moving forward with the case, as is discussed later in this report.

Jurisdictional Lines

For legal purposes, jurisdictional boundaries have been drawn between nations, states, and other localities. Within these territories, various enforcement agencies are designated authority to administer justice. When crimes cross state boundaries in violation of federal law, the states may no longer have sole responsibility for criminal enforcement, and the federal government may claim jurisdiction.[25]

Importantly, laws remain effective *primarily* within the territorial lines of a given jurisdiction. Criminals have long understood this phenomenon—and exploited it. For example, boosters in organized retail crime (ORC) rings[26] may travel across state lines to target various locations of a specific retail establishment in multiple states. They can steal goods from each location, taking just enough to remain under the felony theft level for a given state and thus avoid prosecution for felony theft. In May 2009, for instance, four New York residents were arrested in New Hampshire

---

[23] Testimony by Jason Weinstein, Criminal Division, U.S. Department of Justice, before U.S. Congress, Senate Committee on the Judiciary, Subcommittee on Crime and Terrorism, *Cybersecurity: Responding to the Threat of Cyber Crime and Terrorism*, 112th Cong., 1st sess., April 12, 2011, http://www.justice.gov/criminal/pr/testimony/2011/crm-testimony-110412 html.

[24] Federal Bureau of Investigation, "U.S. Indicts Ohio Man and Two Foreign Residents in Alleged Ukraine-Based 'Scareware' Fraud Scheme That Caused $100 Million in Losses to Internet Victims Worldwide," press release, May 27, 2010, http://chicago fbi.gov/dojpressrel/pressrel10/cg052710 htm. Scareware is fake security software that appears to be legitimate. It misleads users into purchasing fake anti-virus or hard drive cleanup software that may prove to be malicious. For more information, see Gregg Keizer, "Windows Scareware Fakes Impending Drive Disaster," *ComputerWorld*, May 16, 2011, http://www.computerworld.com/s/article/9216765/ Windows_scareware_fakes_impending_drive_disaster?taxonomyId=17.

[25] For more information, see Daniel C. Richman, "The Changing Boundaries Between Federal and Local Law Enforcement," *Boundary Changes in Criminal Justice Organizations*, pp. 81-111, http://www ncjrs.gov/ criminal_justice2000/vol_2/02d2.pdf. For a legal discussion of state sovereignty and federalism issues, see CRS Report RL30315, *Federalism, State Sovereignty, and the Constitution: Basis and Limits of Congressional Power*, by Kenneth R. Thomas.

[26] ORC typically refers to large-scale retail theft and fraud by organized groups of professional shoplifters, or "boosters." A booster is someone who steals merchandise and then sells it to a "fence" for a profit. A fence is someone who knowingly buys illegally obtained goods from a booster and then sells the goods for a profit. For more information on ORC, see CRS Report R41118, *Organized Retail Crime*, by Kristin M. Finklea.

---

for allegedly stealing hair care products from pharmacies. Authorities reportedly found in the suspects' van maps indicating drugstore locations in several East Coast states.[27]

Jurisdictional lines exist not only within the United States, but internationally as well. The United States shares borders with Canada and Mexico, and on each side of these boundaries, sovereign nations govern. A perpetrator committing a crime in the United States may flee across the northern or southern borders (or to another country overseas) to a land where the United States no longer has legal jurisdiction. In one case prosecuted by DOJ, a New Jersey man was convicted in 2005 for his role in a conspiracy to bring heroin to the United States from Colombia. Before he could be sentenced, he fled to Colombia until he was later caught and extradited to the United States in March 2009.[28]

In the United States, jurisdictional battles exist not only between federal and state law enforcement—where these fights may be complicated by federal/state concurrent jurisdiction over a case—but between federal law enforcement agencies themselves. Several agencies have overlapping missions and jurisdictions over the types of cases they may prosecute. For instance, there have been turf disputes between the Federal Bureau of Investigation (FBI) and the Bureau of Alcohol, Tobacco, Firearms, and Explosives (ATF) over cigarette smuggling and explosives cases, among others;[29] between U.S. Immigration and Customs Enforcement (ICE) and ATF over transnational firearms trafficking cases and firearms cases involving unauthorized immigrants;[30] and between ICE and the Drug Enforcement Administration (DEA) over transnational drug trafficking and other cases.[31]

For law enforcement, these struggles to establish programmatic scope may be equally prevalent in the physical and cyber worlds. In both domains, however, agencies can rely, in part, on authorized jurisdictional boundaries to stake claim to their operational turf. And, in the real world, law enforcement can also rely on geographic borders where those borders simultaneously designate jurisdictional lines.

---

[27] "Organized Retail Crime Jumps to 92%," *Retailer Daily*, June 10, 2009, pp. http://www retailerdaily.com/entry/41799/organized-retail-crime-jumps/.

[28] U.S. Department of Justice, "New Jersey Man Sentenced to 13 Years in Federal Prison," press release, June 17, 2010, http://www.justice.gov/usao/ncw/press/mendoza html.

[29] Jerry Markon, "FBI-ATF Turf Battle Hurts Bomb Probes, Official Says," *The Washington Post*, August 27, 2010, http://www.washingtonpost.com/wp-dyn/content/article/2010/08/26/AR2010082606631 html. See also Jerry Markon, "FBI, ATF Battle for Control Of Cases: Cooperation Lags Despite Merger," *Washington Post*, May 10, 2008, http://www.washingtonpost.com/wp-dyn/content/article/2008/05/09/AR2008050903096 html.

[30] U.S. Department of Justice, Office of the Inspector General, *Review of ATF's Project Gunrunner*, I-2011-001, November 2010, http://www.justice.gov/oig/reports/ATF/e1101.pdf. See also U.S. Immigration and Customs Enforcement, "ATF, ICE update partnership agreement to maximize investigative efforts," press release, June 30, 2009, http://www.ice.gov/news/releases/0906/090630albuquerque htm.

[31] See, for example, Joe Palazzolo, "Rival Agencies Agree to Halt Turf Battles," August 10, 2009, http://www.mainjustice.com/2009/08/10/justice-department-and-immigration-and-customs-enforcement-forge-new-partnership/.

Interplay of Borders, Turf, Cyberspace, and Jurisdiction Shaping Crime and Law Enforcement

As mentioned, many 21st century criminals exploit borders and cyberspace in their illicit activities, and they occasionally establish operational turf. In addition, as criminals may clash over their turf, law enforcement, too, can struggle over jurisdiction. Each of these realities presents unique opportunities for criminals and challenges to U.S. law enforcement. Further, the intersection of these elements can potentially compound obstacles to counter-crime efforts.

As seen in **Figure 1**, criminals may operate alone or as part of an extensive network. Without regard for geographic borders or law enforcement jurisdictions, criminals may organize with one another and carry out their illicit activities. Likewise, their operational turf is unconstrained by these lines. Criminals also rely on constantly advancing technology and near anonymity in cyberspace to work both within and across borders and jurisdictions. All the while, law enforcement jurisdiction is often constrained by boundaries—established by jurisdictions and otherwise. Even within a given jurisdictional boundary, multiple agencies may have investigative authority, contributing to possible disagreements over case leadership and control.

Figure 1. Conceptualization of the Operational Universe of Crime and Law Enforcement

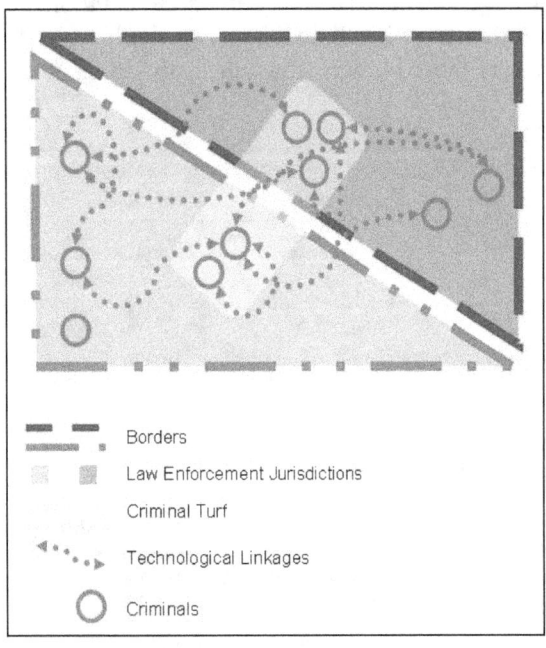

Borders

Law Enforcement Jurisdictions

Criminal Turf

Technological Linkages

○ Criminals

Source: CRS.

Each of the four operational realities within which law enforcement and crime operate (borders, turf, cyberspace, and jurisdictions) also overlap. The following sections analyze selected areas of overlap, highlighting the modern-day opportunities for criminals and challenges to policing. In light of these interwoven realities, law enforcement and policy makers may question how to best design administrative and legislative policies to combat ever-evolving criminal threats.

Physical Borders and Jurisdictional Lines

One author has noted: "Criminal networks thrive on international mobility and their ability to take advantage of the opportunities that flow from the separation of marketplaces into sovereign states with borders."[32] Criminals are proactive, creative, and flexible. They are not constrained by jurisdiction in the same manner as law enforcement. They carry out their illicit activities in spite of geographic lines or

---

[32] Moisés Naím, *Illicit: How Smugglers, Traffickers, and Copycats are Hijacking the Global Economy* (New York: Anchor Books, 2005), p. 13.

jurisdictional boundaries. Criminals routinely move illicit products and proceeds across state and international boundaries.

Criminals have creatively circumvented both geographic borders and law enforcement jurisdictions. Mexican drug traffickers, for instance, utilize underground, cross-border tunnels—which have become increasingly prevalent and sophisticated—to smuggle drugs from Mexico into the United States. Simple "gopher hole" tunnels are dug on the Mexican side of the border, travel just below the surface, and pop out on the U.S. side as close as 100 feet from the border. More advanced tunnels rely on existing infrastructure, such as storm drains or sewage systems. These systems may be shared by neighboring border cities such as the tunnel shared by Nogales, AZ, in the United States and Nogales, Sonora, in Mexico. Exploiting infrastructure allows smugglers to move drugs further than they could by digging tunnels alone. The most sophisticated tunnels can have rail, ventilation, and electrical systems. The most extensive of such tunnels discovered to date were found in January 2006 in Otay Mesa, CA. They stretched nearly three-quarters of a mile in length, traveled over 85 feet below the surface of the earth, and had lighting, ventilation, and groundwater drainage systems.[33] In November 2010, the San Diego Tunnel Task Force[34] uncovered two similar tunnels running between Tijuana, Mexico, and Otay Mesa, CA.[35]

Traffickers have also used semi-submersible maritime vessels, ultralight aircraft,[36] and other means to move illicit products. Semi-submersible vessels are typically made of fiberglass, can travel up to 2,000 miles with multi-ton shipments of drugs—primarily Colombian cocaine—and are difficult to detect from the air.[37] The U.S. Coast Guard has indicated that over 25% of the cocaine eventually destined for the United States is moved during part of its journey via semi-submersible vessels.[38] Mexican drug traffickers have increasingly used ultralight aircraft to smuggle drugs across the Southwest border. These small planes can fly as low as tree level and are not easily detected. Some traffickers land the ultralights on the U.S. side of the border to pass off drug loads to distributors. Others attach drop baskets[39] to release packages of drugs that will fall to the ground when a lever in the aircraft is activated. These packages are then picked up and distributed by local traffickers or gangs. In FY2010, border authorities reported 228 ultralight

---

[33] This tunnel bust resulted in the seizure of more than two tons of marijuana. U.S. Drug Enforcement Administration, "DEA/ICE Uncover 'Massive' Cross-Border Drug Tunnel, Cement lined passage thought to link warehouses in Tijuana and Otay Mesa," press release, January 26, 2006, http://www.justice.gov/dea/pubs/pressrel/pr012606 html.

[34] This Task Force was created in 2003 as a partnership between ICE, DEA, and the USBP, along with state law enforcement and Mexican counterparts.

[35] U.S. Drug Enforcement Administration, "Discovery of 2nd Major San Diego-Area Cross-Border Drug Tunnel Leads to 8 Arrests, Seizure of More Than 20 Tons of Marijuana," press release, November 26, 2010, http://www.justice.gov/dea/pubs/states/newsrel/2010/sd112610.html.

[36] The Federal Aviation Administration (FAA) does not classify ultralights as "aircraft." For the FAA definition of an ultralight, see the Code of Federal Regulations (CFR) Title 14, Section 103, http://ecfr.gpoaccess.gov/cgi/t/text/text-idx?c=ecfr&sid=77f64066b8e425c01339f918e6e9f291&rgn=div5&view=text&node=14:2.0.1.3.16&idno=14.

[37] "Self-Propelled Semi-Submersible (SPSS) Watercraft," *GlobalSecurity.org*, June 28, 2008, http://www.globalsecurity.org/military/world/para/spss htm. See also "Waving, Not Drowning: Cocaine Now Moves by Submarine," *The Economist*, May 1, 2008, http://www.economist.com/node/11294435?story_id=11294435.

[38] Rear Admiral Vincent Atkins, U.S. Coast Guard, Testimony before the House Subcommittee on Homeland Security, on Department of Homeland Security Air and Marine Operations and Investments, April 19, 2010, http://www.dhs.gov/ynews/testimony/testimony_1271690315007.shtm.

[39] Drop baskets can carry over 300 pounds of marijuana or other drugs.

---

incursions from Mexico into the United States—nearly double the number reported from FY2009.[40]

Smugglers and traffickers are constantly innovating means to circumvent borders and supply their products to areas where there is demand. In January 2010, smugglers along the Southwest border were intercepted in Mexico as they prepared a catapult device equipped to fling 4.4-pound packages of marijuana over the fence along the international border between Mexico and the United States.[41] While the attempt was unsuccessful—the drugs and catapult were both seized by authorities—this highlights criminal will to overcome physical, legal, and other barriers to generating profit. In another instance, in April 2010, smugglers used a portable folding ramp mounted on a truck to allow vehicles to drive over the international border fence. U.S. Border Patrol agents spotted a vehicle that had used this ramp and seized 1,000 pounds of marijuana after the suspects abandoned their vehicle and fled back to Mexico.[42]

While many scholars believe that borders present opportunities for criminals, others have noted challenges. Criminals may be able to establish roots in new territory if there "is the presence of a demand for criminal protection in the new place. The presence of large illegal markets, booms in construction, an export-oriented economy, incentives to create cartel agreements, or the inability of the state to settle legal disputes quickly and effectively usually generate such a demand."[43] In fact, criminal organizations may expand into new territories by force rather than by choice. They may be moving to escape criminal infighting, turf battles, or effective law enforcement.[44]

Challenges for U.S. Law Enforcement

While criminals may operate across jurisdictional boundaries, law enforcement cannot. As mentioned, jurisdictional lines generally follow territorial lines, and U.S. federal law enforcement may investigate and prosecute qualifying federal crimes within the territorial confines of the United States. For a given crime, federal law enforcement may be able to pursue an investigation provided that the criminal act, criminal actors, and victims are all within the United States. However, many crimes—particularly those of the cyber nature—have become increasingly transnational. While Congress has provided federal law enforcement extraterritorial jurisdiction for certain crimes, this does not necessarily clear law enforcement's path to engage in such investigations.[45]

---

[40] Richard Marosi, "Ultralight Aircraft Now Ferrying Drugs Across U.S.-Mexico Border," *Los Angeles Times*, May 19, 2011, http://www.latimes.com/news/local/la-me-border-ultralight-20110520,0,7315999.story.

[41] "Mexican Drug Cartels Use Catapult to Launch Drug Packages Across Border," *Homeland Security Newswire*, January 27, 2011, http://homelandsecuritynewswire.com/mexican-drug-cartels-use-catapult-launch-drug-packages-across-border.

[42] "Smugglers Use Portable Ramp to Jump Border Fence," *Homeland Security Newswire*, April 19, 2011, http://homelandsecuritynewswire.com/smugglers-use-portable-ramp-jump-border-fence. See also Chris McDaniel, "Smugglers Improvise Ramp to Drive Over Border Fence," *Yuma Sun*, April 8, 2011, http://www.yumasun.com/articles/border-69033-fence-ramp.html.

[43] Federico Varese, *Mafias on the Move: How Organized Crime Conquers New Territories* (Princeton, NJ: Princeton University Press, 2011), pp. 7-8.

[44] Ibid. p. 8.

[45] For a detailed discussion of extraterritorial jurisdiction, see CRS Report 94-166, *Extraterritorial Application of American Criminal Law*, by Charles Doyle.

Perhaps an alleged criminal committed a crime within the United States and then fled the country to evade prosecution. Or, perhaps a criminal targeted U.S. persons, businesses, or interests from outside U.S. territorial bounds. The United States may have to rely on other countries' law enforcement to assist in a criminal investigation or to help extradite suspected criminals to face prosecution in the United States.[46] One such barrier to investigation and prosecution exists when the United States does not have an extradition or legal assistance arrangement with the country in which a fugitive has found haven.[47] Even if there is an extradition treaty, however, extradition can be complicated for a number of reasons. For one, an illegal action in one country may not be prohibited in another.[48] This could contribute to one country's reluctance to work with another or to turn over a suspect for prosecution. In the United States, for example, creating, possessing, and distributing child pornography are illegal; this is not the case, however, in a number of other countries. A 2006 study by the International Center for Missing and Exploited Children found that of 184 International Criminal Police Organization (INTERPOL) member countries, 95 countries had no laws criminalizing child pornography.[49]

The disparity between countries' cybercrime laws has been cited as another obstacle to investigations. Law enforcement has used the investigation of the "Love Bug," or "I Love You," computer virus as a prominent example of this barrier.[50] This virus was unleashed in the Philippines, and it attacked computers worldwide, including in Asia, Europe, Australia, and the United States. The creator of the virus, although arrested, was not charged with a crime because Philippine law at the time was not sufficient to address hacking and computer crimes.[51]

In addition to the challenges posed by investigating transnational criminals, impediments exist for U.S. law enforcement in combating criminals crossing boundaries within the territorial United States. The prevention and control of domestic crime has traditionally been a responsibility of state and local governments, with the federal government playing more of a supportive role. However, between the mid-1980s and mid-1990s, federal law enforcement agencies saw an expansion of their role in fighting domestic crime as Congress began to add more crimes to the federal criminal code that were previously under the sole jurisdiction of state and local governments. While the federalization of crimes has increased, criminals can commit any number

---

[46] The Cybersecurity Act of 2012 (S. 2105, S. 3414) would, among other things, require the Attorney General and the Director of the FBI to submit a report to Congress regarding DOJ investigations and prosecutions relating to cybercrimes and intrusions; this report would be required to contain information on the number of arrests and prosecutions related to cybercrimes, instances in which investigations or prosecutions have been hampered by an inability to extradite the suspected criminal, manpower and financial resources devoted to combating cybercrimes, and legal impediments (both domestic and international) to prosecuting cybercrimes and intrusions.

[47] For a list of countries with which the United States has an extradition agreement, see 18 U.S.C. §3181. The United States maintains diplomatic relations with a number of countries with which it does not share an extradition treaty. For instance, while the United States has diplomatic relations with China and Russia, it does not share extradition treaties with these nations.

[48] U.S. Government Accountability Office, *Cybercrime: Public and Private Entities Face Challenges in Addressing Cyber Threats*, GAO-07-705, June 2007, p. 41, http://www.gao.gov/new.items/d07705.pdf.

[49] International Center for Missing and Exploited Children (ICMEC), *Results of the Global Child Pornography Study*, 2006, http://www.icmec.org/en_X1/pdf/SummerNewsletter2006formatted.pdf. ICMEC is a nonprofit organization based in Virginia whose goal is to protect children from sexual exploitation and abduction.

[50] U.S. Department of Justice, "Remarks of Kevin DiGregory, Fighting Cybercrime—What are the Challenges facing Europe?," press release, September 19, 2000, http://www.justice.gov/criminal/cybercrime/EUremarks htm.

[51] The Philippine Congress subsequently passed a law specifically dealing with computer-related crimes. Wayne Arnold, "Philippines to Drop Charges on E-Mail Virus," *The New York Times*, August 22, 2000, http://www.nytimes.com/2000/08/22/business/technology-philippines-to-drop-charges-on-e-mail-virus html.

---

of crimes domestically that are investigated primarily under the purview of state and local law enforcement.[52]

Organized retail crime (ORC), for example, is often multi-jurisdictional. Retail criminals may operate freely across state lines, stealing just enough merchandise to remain under the major theft limit. Theft laws vary from state to state regarding the monetary threshold that constitutes major theft. There is currently no federal law specifically prohibiting organized retail crime as such, but there are provisions in the law that federal law enforcement uses to bring forth cases against ORC rings.[53] For crimes such as ORC that frequently cross borders, Congress has debated whether current law should be amended to provide provisions specifically criminalizing this activity. In this debate surrounding ORC, for instance, proponents of such legislation argue that criminalizing ORC may benefit law enforcement in several ways, including (1) illuminating the growing problem of ORC and (2) providing a statutory framework for tracking ORC case data rather than lumping these cases into other categories for statistical purposes. Opponents of legislation criminalizing ORC argue that already-existing statutes allow for effective investigation and prosecution of ORC and that creating a separate provision for ORC would be redundant. Indeed, representatives from federal law enforcement agencies have provided congressional testimony indicating that they have sufficient laws and procedural tools to investigate ORC.[54]

This highlights a larger federal debate regarding the federalization of offenses. In light of increasingly trans-border crimes, Congress may be faced with deciding whether these offenses are best criminalized at the state or federal level. One factor that may strongly influence this debate is whether state and local law enforcement agencies are equipped with the needed tools and authorities to keep up with savvy criminals who are constantly devising new means to profit and evade the law. One alternative to federalizing offenses is to provide state and local law enforcement with assistance—monetary, manpower, or technological. Congress has provided such assistance through funding grant programs such as the Community Oriented Policing Services (COPS) grant program[55] and the Edward Byrne Memorial Justice Assistance Grant (JAG) program.[56] Through these programs, state and local law enforcement assistance is available for a variety of purpose areas. Yet another option that Congress may consider is incentivizing federal, state, and local law enforcement coordination and information sharing through the participation in task forces and fusion centers. The issue of law enforcement coordination is discussed further in the section "Interagency Cooperation and Information Sharing."

---

[52] For more information on federal crime control issues, see CRS Report R40812, *Federal Crime Control Issues in the 111th Congress*, by Kristin M. Finklea.

[53] These include statutes such as the Racketeer Influenced and Corrupt Organizations (RICO) provisions, money laundering, and transportation or sale of stolen goods provisions.

[54] Testimony by law enforcement representatives from the FBI, ICE, USSS, and USPIS before the U.S. Congress, House Committee on the Judiciary, Subcommittee on Crime, Terrorism, and Homeland Security, *Combating Organized Retail Crime: The Role of Federal Law Enforcement*, 111th Cong., 1st sess., November 5, 2009.

[55] For more information on COPS, see CRS Report RL33308, *Community Oriented Policing Services (COPS): Background and Funding*, by Nathan James; and CRS Report R40709, *Community Oriented Policing Services (COPS): Current Legislative Issues*, by Nathan James.

[56] For more information on JAG, see CRS Report RS22416, *Edward Byrne Memorial Justice Assistance Grant (JAG) Program*, by Nathan James.

Cyberspace and Advancing Technologies

Globalization and technological innovation have fostered the expansion of criminal (and legitimate) operations across physical borders as well as throughout cyberspace. Advanced, rapid communication systems have made it easier for criminals to operate remotely not only from other members of their illicit networks, but from their victims as well.

Cross-Border Criminal Networks

Criminal organizations have evolved to be more networked and cellular than their hierarchical predecessors.[57] Criminals operating as part of a network no longer need to live in the same city, state, or even country as one another. Various components of an organization may perform specific roles that need not be carried out in the same locality in which other members of the illicit network operate. As criminals take on more specialized roles, organizations may outsource portions of their operations to specialists. Specialists can be incorporated into a criminal scheme from all corners of the globe, and opportunistic networks may form around specific schemes. According to the U.S. Secret Service (USSS), "more exclusive online groups [of criminals] count among their members professional criminals who have a decade or more of experience and extensive contacts in diverse criminal communities."[58] Web-based criminal forums, for instance, have global membership, many with "strong representation of members from Eastern Europe."[59] Some of these online forums act as business platforms where members of criminal communities can gather virtually to share and market their expertise.[60] One such forum was known as CarderPlanet, founded by Vladislav Horohorin, or "BadB." While CarderPlanet shut down after law enforcement arrested several high-level members,[61] Horohorin's criminal network "remains one of the most sophisticated organizations of online financial criminals in the world."[62]

As a byproduct of this organizational structure, one component of the network may have limited knowledge of the activities of other members of the network. Therefore, if one component is disrupted by law enforcement, other components of the network may be shielded by the loose organizational structure. While this may protect an organization from being wholly dismantled, it can potentially limit information sharing *within* an organization. This can subsequently stunt the sharing of key communications necessary for organizational learning and growth.[63] Indirectly, the

---

[57] For more information on the evolution of organized crime, see CRS Report R41547, *Organized Crime: An Evolving Challenge for U.S. Law Enforcement*, by Jerome P. Bjelopera and Kristin M. Finklea.

[58] Verizon RISK Team and U.S. Secret Service, *2010 Data Breach Investigations Report*, p. 58.

[59] Ibid.

[60] The USSS has identified some specialized roles as carders who traffic and exploit stolen financial data, hackers and security technologists, spammers, bot herders, money launderers, internet developers and host providers, malware developers, document forgers, information service providers, hardware providers, calling services, and drop/money mule managers. Ibid., p. 59.

[61] Kimberly Kiefer Peretti, *Data Breaches: What the Underground World of "Carding" Reveals*, U.S. Department of Justice, Computer Crime and Intellectual Property Section, p. 9, http://www.justice.gov/criminal/cybercrime/DataBreachesArticle.pdf.

[62] U.S. Department of Justice, "Alleged International Credit Card Trafficker Arrested in France on U.S. Charges Related to Sale of Stolen Card Data," press release, August 11, 2010, http://www.justice.gov/opa/pr/2010/August/10-crm-921.html.

[63] Michael Kenney, *From Pablo to Osama: Trafficking and Terrorist Networks, Government Bureaucracies, and Competitive Adaptation* (University Park, PA: The Pennsylvania State University Press, 2007), p. 5. Hereinafter: Kenney, *From Pablo to Osama.*

---

cellular, networked structures that criminals have adapted and that, in part, allow them to more effectively operate across borders can hinder their internal operations and potential growth.

This phenomenon is not exclusive to criminal organizations, however. While there has been a trend towards increased information sharing in the law enforcement community—particularly since the terrorist attacks of September 11, 2001—compartmentalization still exists.[64] Agencies have adopted more intelligence-led investigations, but they still compartmentalize their operations and restrict information on a need-to-know basis.[65] In this fashion, they also put up barriers to potential organizational growth and learning. Some have suggested that while criminals and police both compartmentalize information, the means and speed with which they ultimately share information may differ. One scholar has analyzed this phenomenon in the context of smuggling networks, noting that they "often process information, make decisions, coordinate behavior, and change practices faster than the cumbersome bureaucracies that confront them."[66]

Trans-border Victimization

Not only do criminals operate and network with one another across borders, but criminals (both individuals and organizations) often target victims without regard for borders. According to the Internet Crime Complaint Center (IC3),[67] of those reported scams and frauds from 2010 where the locations of the victim and perpetrator were both known, a minority of cases involved victims and perpetrators in the same state.[68] For instance, in California (the state with the largest proportion of victims and perpetrators reportedly in the same state), 39.1% of cases with known location information indicated that the victim and perpetrator were both located in California. Anonymity in the cyber world helps criminals operate with relative freedom. In addition, criminals may operate under numerous identities—actual, stolen, or cyber—that can link them to different parts of the world, confounding victims and law enforcement alike.

Modern criminals can readily leverage technology to victimize targets across borders. They can rely upon botnets,[69] for instance, to electronically target victims throughout borderless cyberspace. Simultaneously, the criminals themselves need not cross a single border. The Coreflood botnet, for one, has infected over 2.3 million computers around the world—almost 1.9 million of which are located in the United States.[70] This botnet, or virus, is a malicious keylogging program that records users' keystrokes and transmits the data to cyber thieves, who can use these data to steal personal and financial information. Compromised U.S. businesses suffering financial losses from the botnet range from real estate and investment companies to law firms and defense contractors. The FBI has filed a complaint against 13 "John Doe" defendants

---

[64] For more information on intelligence sharing, see CRS Report R41848, *Intelligence Information: Need-to-Know vs. Need-to-Share*, by Richard F. Grimmett.

[65] Ibid. See also Kenney, *From Pablo to Osama*, p. 7, 103.

[66] Kenney, *From Pablo to Osama*, p. 7.

[67] The FBI partners with the National White Collar Crime Center (NW3C) to form the IC3. The IC3 serves the broad law enforcement community to receive, develop, and refer internet crime complaints.

[68] Internet Crime Complaint Center, *2010 Internet Crime Report*, p. 9, http://ic3report nw3c.org/docs/2010_IC3_Report_02_10_11_low_res.pdf.

[69] Botnets are groups of computers that are remotely controlled by hackers. They have been infected by downloading malicious software and are used to carry out malicious activities on behalf of the hackers.

[70] *U.S. v. John Doe*, Complaint, April 11, 2011, U.S. District Court of Connecticut, http://newhaven.fbi.gov/dojpressrel/pressrel11/pdf/nh041311_4.pdf.

---

believed to have engaged in wire fraud, bank fraud, and illegal interception of electronic communications in connection with the Coreflood botnet.[71] It is unknown whether authorities have determined the exact identities or locations of these alleged criminals, but they are believed to be foreign nationals.[72] Notably, authorities in the United States and Estonia have seized servers that are believed to have current, or have had previous, control over the Coreflood botnet.[73]

Advance fee fraud (AFF) schemes have, even before the proliferation of the internet, been used to swindle victims across borders. The internet has only hastened the speed with which these fraudsters can reach their targets and increased the number of potential victims. AFF scams often involve criminals sending unsolicited, or spam, e-mails that present an opportunity for a "lucky" individual to come into a large sum of money.[74] The letters promise the money will be disbursed once the victim sends a small cash payment, purportedly used to facilitate the transfer. Only, the large sum of money is never transferred to the victim. In one case from February 2011, the second of two Nigerian nationals was sentenced to nine years in prison for his role in an AFF scheme targeting U.S., European, and Australian individuals.[75] At least 18 people were duped out of over $9.5 million. The fraudsters posed as lawyers, bankers, and government officials who collected the "fees" that were advertised as necessary to secure the transfer of large sums of money to the victims. Of course, the victims never received their promised riches. The perpetrators were eventually arrested in the Netherlands (where they had been residing) and extradited to the United States.

The internet has also been used to perpetuate trans-border intellectual property rights (IPR) violations—one of the primary cybercrime concerns voiced by federal law enforcement and the Obama Administration.[76] Counterfeit and pirated goods harm legitimate businesses and consumers on several levels. This crime threatens competition and innovation, siphons profits deserved by the rightful manufacturer, and poses health risks to consumers. In June 2011, a Chinese national was sentenced for trafficking in counterfeit versions of the pharmaceutical weight-loss drug "Alli"—an over-the-counter weight-loss drug manufactured by GlaxoSmithKlein. The defendant reportedly shipped the products from China to a business partner in Texas for U.S. distribution. The FDA had issued public alerts about this as well as other supposed weight-loss products.[77] The warnings indicated that the counterfeit drugs were being

---

[71] Federal Bureau of Investigation, "Department of Justice Takes Action to Disable International Botnet: More Than Two Million Computers Infected with Keylogging Software as Part of Massive Fraud Scheme," press release, April 13, 2011, http://newhaven fbi.gov/dojpressrel/pressrel11/nh041311 htm.

[72] *U.S. v. John Doe*, Complaint, April 11, 2011, U.S. District Court of Connecticut, http://newhaven.fbi.gov/dojpressrel/pressrel11/pdf/nh041311_4.pdf.

[73] Kim Zetter, "FBI vs. Coreflood Botnet: Round 1 Goes to the Feds," *Wired.com*, April 26, 2011, http://www.wired.com/threatlevel/2011/04/coreflood_results/.

[74] Federal Bureau of Investigation, "Common Fraud Schemes," http://www.fbi.gov/majcases/fraud/fraudschemes htm. For more information on the development of AFF scams, see CRS Report R41547, *Organized Crime: An Evolving Challenge for U.S. Law Enforcement*, by Jerome P. Bjelopera and Kristin M. Finklea.

[75] U.S. Department of Justice, "Nigerian National Sentenced in North Carolina to 108 Months in Prison for Role in Advance Fee Fraud Scheme," press release, February 24, 2011, http://www.justice.gov/opa/pr/2011/February/11-crm-242 html.

[76] See Federal Bureau of Investigation, "Gordon M. Snow, Assistant Director, Cyber Division, Federal Bureau of Investigation, Statement Before the Senate Judiciary Committee, Subcommittee on Crime and Terrorism," April 11, 2011, http://www.fbi.gov/news/testimony/cybersecurity-responding-to-the-threat-of-cyber-crime-and-terrorism. See also White House, *International Strategy for Cyberspace: Prosperity, Security, and Openness in a Networked World*, May 2011, p. 4, http://www.whitehouse.gov/sites/default/files/rss_viewer/international_strategy_for_cyberspace.pdf.

[77] U.S. Immigration and Customs Enforcement, "Chinese National Sentenced to More Than 7 Years in Federal Prison (continued...)

---

imported from China and that the "counterfeit version [of Alli] did not contain orlistat, the active ingredient in its product. Instead, the counterfeit product contained the controlled substance sibutramine." One consumer was even reported to have suffered a mild stroke after consuming the counterfeit product.[78] Over the course of the investigation, law enforcement purchased the counterfeit drug and traced the wired money used in the purchase of the counterfeit drug. They located the defendant in China and, posing as potential buyers of the drug, agreed to meet the defendant face-to-face. Law enforcement later met the defendant in Hawaii, where he was arrested.[79]

Barriers to Cyber Investigations

Many of law enforcement's barriers in the cyber world have a technological dimension rather than being purely jurisdictional. Police agencies face challenges in identifying and prosecuting criminals[80] who can operate under a variety of identities, including cyber identities that can be instantaneously altered, and who can conduct operations throughout the world without regard for borders (of which law enforcement is acutely aware). According to the FBI, "cyber criminals routinely change their nicknames, e-mails, digital currency accounts, and the ICQ [or instant messaging] numbers they use in forums. Not only do they change these accounts and identifying numbers, but they also use different combinations of the information in each forum they participate in."[81]

Location of Crimes and Criminals

Cybercriminals often target victims in one or more different countries. Further, given the nature of the cyber world, crimes can be routed through servers in countries entirely separate from those where the perpetrators and victims are located. The Financial Action Task Force (FATF) has indicated that "it appears that the perpetrators take advantage of the near anonymity that can sometimes be achieved through internet communication on the internet, as well as the difficulty in following the path of communication links from one internet server to another."[82]

(...continued)

for Trafficking Counterfeit Pharmaceutical Weight-Loss Drug," press release, June 3, 2011, http://www.ice.gov/news/releases/1106/110603denver htm.

[78] U.S. Immigration and Customs Enforcement, "Chinese National Sentenced to More Than 7 Years in Federal Prison for Trafficking Counterfeit Pharmaceutical Weight-Loss Drug," press release, June 3, 2011, http://www.ice.gov/news/releases/1106/110603denver htm.

[79] U.S. Food and Drug Administration, "FDA Warns Consumers about Counterfeit Alli," press release, January 18, 2010, http://www.fda.gov/NewsEvents/Newsroom/PressAnnouncements/ucm197857 htm.

[80] The Cybersecurity Act of 2012 (S. 2105, S. 3414) would, among other things, require the Attorney General and the Director of the FBI to submit a report to Congress regarding DOJ investigations and prosecutions relating to cybercrimes and intrusions; this report would be required to contain information on the number of arrests and prosecutions related to cybercrimes, instances in which investigations or prosecutions have been hampered by an inability to extradite the suspected criminal, manpower and financial resources devoted to combating cybercrimes, and legal impediments (both domestic and international) to prosecuting cybercrimes and intrusions.

[81] Federal Bureau of Investigation, Steven R. Chabinsky, Deputy Assistant Director, Cyber Division at the GovSec/FOSE Conference, March 23, 2010, http://www.fbi.gov/news/speeches/the-cyber-threat-whos-doing-what-to-whom.

[82] Financial Action Task Force on Money Laundering, *Report on Money Laundering Typologies: 2000 - 2001*, February 1, 2001, p. 3, http://www fatf-gafi.org/dataoecd/29/36/34038090.pdf.

The Rustock botnet, for example, was a vast network of computers—estimated at over 1 million computers around the world—that sent malicious spam.[83] Reports indicate that this botnet may have been responsible for over half of worldwide spam at the end of 2010. "Command-and-control" machines, responsible for sending instructions to the other infected computers, were located primarily in the United States. Microsoft worked with the U.S. Marshals Service and the Dutch High Tech Crime Unit in the Netherlands to dismantle the command-and-control structure.[84] In another case, from December 2010, DOJ arraigned a Russian national with the cyber identity "AKILL," who was the reported ringleader of the Mega-D botnet.[85] This botnet could send 10 billion e-mails daily. AKILL supposedly falsified the e-mail header information to disguise the e-mails' true origins. One technique to enhance anonymity used by botnet leaders, or botmasters, is to launder their internet traffic through a variety of intermediate internet hosts, protocols, and anonymous networks. Similar to money laundering, this traffic laundering makes it increasingly difficult for law enforcement to detect the source of the malicious botnet activity.[86]

Same Crimes, Advanced Technologies

Criminals exploit rapidly evolving technology to stay ahead of law enforcement. Internet technology is used not only in the furtherance of cybercrimes, but in more traditional, real world crimes as well. According to Europol's 2011 Organized Crime Threat Assessment,

> Internet technology has now emerged as a key facilitator for the vast majority of offline organised crime activity. In addition to the high-tech crimes of cybercrime, payment card fraud, the distribution of child abuse material, and audio visual piracy, extensive use of the Internet now underpins illicit drug synthesis, extraction and distribution, the recruitment and marketing of victims of trafficking in human beings (THB), the facilitation of illegal immigration, the supply of counterfeit commodities, trafficking in endangered species, and many other criminal activities. It is also widely used as a secure communication and money laundering tool by criminal groups.[87]

While criminals are proactively searching for new techniques to accomplish the same crimes and generate money, law enforcement is reacting to criminals' activities. Take, for instance, advances in the movement of illegal drug trafficking proceeds across the U.S. border with Mexico. While bulk cash smuggling has been an important means by which criminals have moved illegal profits from the United States into Mexico, traffickers have increasingly turned to stored-value cards to move money.

---

[83] Nick Wingfield, "Spam Network Shut Down," *WSJ.com*, March 18, 2011, http://online.wsj.com/article/SB10001424052748703328404576207173861008758 html?KEYWORDS=nick+wingfield.

[84] Microsoft, "Taking Down Botnets: Microsoft and the Rustock Botnet," March 17, 2011, http://blogs.technet.com/b/microsoft_on_the_issues/archive/2011/03/18/taking-down-botnets-microsoft-and-the-rustock-botnet.aspx.

[85] U.S. Department of Justice, "Russian Man Charged with Sending Thousands of Spam Emails," press release, December 3, 2010, http://www.justice.gov/usao/wie/press_releases/2010/pr20101203_Russian_Press_release.pdf.

[86] Xinyuan Wang and Daniel Ramsbrock, "The Botnet Problem," *Computer and Information Security Handbook*, ed. John R. Vacca (Elsevier Inc., 2009), p. 129.

[87] Europol, *EU Organized Threat Assessment: OCTA 2011*, File No. 2530-274, April 28, 2011, p. 6, http://www.europol.europa.eu/publications/European_Organised_Crime_Threat_Assessment_%28OCTA%29/OCTA_2011.pdf.

With these cards, criminals are able to avoid the reporting requirement under which they would have to declare any amount over $10,000 in cash moving across the border.[88] Current federal regulations regarding international transportation only apply to monetary instruments as defined under the Bank Secrecy Act (BSA).[89] Of note, a stored-value card is not currently considered a monetary instrument under current law. These transportation regulations indicate that

> Each person who physically transports, mails, or ships, or causes to be physically transported, mailed, or shipped, or attempts to physically transport, mail or ship, or attempts to cause to be physically transported, mailed or shipped, currency or other monetary instruments in an aggregate amount exceeding $10,000 at one time from the United States to any place outside the United States, or into the United States from any place outside the United States, shall make a report thereof. A person is deemed to have caused such transportation, mailing or shipping when he aids, abets, counsels, commands, procures, or requests it to be done by a financial institution or any other person.[90]

The Financial Crimes Enforcement Network (FinCEN)[91] has issued a final rule, defining "stored value" as "prepaid access" and implementing regulations regarding the recordkeeping and suspicious activity reporting requirements for prepaid access products and services.[92] The rule does not, however, directly address whether stored value or prepaid access cards would be subject to current regulations regarding the international transportation of monetary instruments. Even if FinCEN were to implement regulations requiring individuals leaving the United States to declare stored value, the Government Accountability Office (GAO) has identified several challenges that would remain.[93] These challenges relate to law enforcement's ability to detect the actual cards and to differentiate legitimate from illegitimate stored value on cards; travelers' abilities to remember the amount of stored value on any given card; and law enforcement's ability to determine where illegitimate stored value is physically held and subsequently freeze and seize the assets.

Aside from bulk cash smuggling and stored-value cards, traffickers move and launder money by using digital currency accounts, e-businesses that facilitate money transfers via the internet, online role-playing games or virtual worlds that enable the exchange of game-based currencies for real currency, and mobile banking wherein traffickers have remote access—via cell phones—to bank and credit card accounts as well as prepaid cards.[94]

---

[88] Legislation was introduced in the 111th Congress (H.R. 5127) that would have, among other things, classified stored-value cards as monetary instruments in order to require individuals to declare to Customs over $10,000 that they are carrying on a stored value card.

[89] 31 U.S.C. §5312(a)(3) defines a monetary instrument as "(A) United States coins and currency; (B) as the Secretary may prescribe by regulation, coins and currency of a foreign country, travelers' checks, bearer negotiable instruments, bearer investment securities, bearer securities, stock on which title is passed on delivery, and similar material; and (C) as the Secretary of the Treasury shall provide by regulation for purposes of sections 5316 and 5331 , checks, drafts, notes, money orders, and other similar instruments which are drawn on or by a foreign financial institution and are not in bearer form."

[90] 31 C.F.R. §103.23(a).

[91] FinCEN, under the Department of the Treasury, administers the BSA and the nation's financial intelligence unit. FinCEN also supports law enforcement, intelligence, and regulatory agencies by analyzing and sharing financial intelligence information. For more information, see http://www.fincen.gov/about_fincen/wwd/strategic.html.

[92] Department of the Treasury, Financial Crimes Enforcement Network, "Bank Secrecy Act Regulations—Definitions and Other Regulations Relating to Prepaid Access," 76, No. 146 *Federal Register* 45403-45420, July 29, 2011.

[93] GAO, *Moving Illegal Proceeds: Challenges Exist in the Federal Government's Effort to Stem Cross Border Smuggling*, October 2010, pp. 48–49.

[94] Douglas Farah, "Money Laundering and Bulk Cash Smuggling: Challenges for the Merida Initiative," in *Shared* (continued...)

Technology Outpacing Law Enforcement

Savvy criminals can evade law enforcement because they use, at times, technology and methods that are beyond the reach and expertise of law enforcement. In the rapidly evolving digital age, law enforcement may not have the capabilities to keep up with the pace of criminals. For instance, law enforcement specialists face mounting challenges in gathering information protected by sophisticated encryption.[95] Criminals can use data encryption software to mask electronic communications—sending information to undisclosed locations and individuals. While law enforcement may be able to intercept these data, they may not have the tools to crack the encryption and obtain valuable evidence.[96] This could potentially contribute to large amounts of data that can be collected but not analyzed.

The FBI has described a problem that results from a gap between investigative authority and capability. While law enforcement has the legal authority to conduct electronic surveillance and wiretaps, investigators may not be able to utilize these techniques if communications providers' technologies (or lack thereof) prevent law enforcement from implementing their legal authorities.[97] In essence, the FBI may be "'in the dark' by the loss of evidence, that [they] would be lawfully entitled to, due to advances in technology, antiquated ELSUR [electronic surveillance] laws, and or lack of resources, training, personnel."[98] As such, the FBI has created the "Going Dark" initiative (discussed later), which "is a National Electronic Surveillance Strategy which focuses on law enforcement's impending inability to conduct electronic surveillance on certain communications devices due to rapid changes in technology."[99]

Not only can criminals' innovation and use of technology outpace law enforcement's investigations, but the relative costs to criminals and law enforcement appear to be unbalanced as well. Technology leveraged by criminals can be relatively low-cost.[100] In comparison, the costs to investigate these crimes—in terms of both financial and personnel resource costs—can be higher.

(...continued)

Responsibility: U.S.-Mexico Policy Options for Confronting Organized Crime, ed. Eric L. Olson, David A. Shirk, and Andrew D. Selee (2010).

[95] See archived CRS Report 98-905, *The Encryption Debate: Intelligence Aspects*, by Keith G. Tidball and Richard A. Best Jr.

[96] Microsoft has created a tool to help law enforcement overcome some barriers posed by its data encryption tool, BitLocker. The Computer Online Forensic Evidence Extractor (COFEE) can help law enforcement capture live data on a computer. The tool ceases to work, however, if the computer is shut down. Nancy Gohring, "Microsoft Helps Law Enforcement Get Around Encryption," *PCWorld*, April 29, 2008, http://www.pcworld.com/businesscenter/article/145318/microsoft_helps_law_enforcement_get_around_encryption html.

[97] Federal Bureau of Investigation, "Valerie Caproni, General Counsel, Statement Before the House Judiciary Committee, Subcommittee on Crime, Terrorism, and Homeland Security," February 17, 2011, http://www.fbi.gov/news/testimony/going-dark-lawful-electronic-surveillance-in-the-face-of-new-technologies.

[98] See Freedom of Information Act (FOIA) documents provided by the FBI to the Electronic Frontier Foundation (EFF), p. 120, http://www.eff.org/files/20110207_FBI_Going_Dark_Release_Part_4.pdf. Links to the all relevant FOIA documents provided to the EFF are referenced by Jennifer Lynch, "Newly Released Documents Detail FBI's Plan to Expand Federal Surveillance Laws," *Electronic Frontier Foundation*, February 15, 2011, http://www.eff.org/deeplinks/2011/02/newly-released-documents-detail-fbi-s-plan-expand.

[99] See Freedom of Information Act (FOIA) documents provided by the FBI to the Electronic Frontier Foundation (EFF), p. 110, http://www.eff.org/files/20110207_FBI_Going_Dark_Release_Part_4.pdf.

[100] Phil Williams, "Transnational Criminal Networks," in *Networks and Netwars: The Future of Terror, Crime, and Military*, ed. John Arquilla and David Ronfeldt (RAND, 2001), p. 82.

Jurisdictional Battles

Establishing, maintaining, and expanding operational turf can all pose challenges to criminals. Criminals open themselves to increased exposure—to rival actors and law enforcement alike—when efforts to stake claim to and defend turf occur in the open. Criminals generally do not strive to publicize their illicit activities. In effect, this is a key element that separates criminals from terrorists. Criminals are often motivated by profit. They try to keep their activities under wraps without letting their identities be known. This anonymity increases the likelihood that they will be able to continue their activities without detection.

As noted, criminals operate with relative ease across borders. They have connections and trusted networks in different geographic areas. For instance, in order to facilitate the distribution and sale of drugs in the United States, Mexican DTOs have formed relationships with U.S. street gangs, prison gangs, and outlaw motorcycle gangs.[101] While criminals may work through fluid trans-border alliances, law enforcement may not have parallel partnerships in each of the jurisdictional areas where criminal networks operate. Thus, criminals may be shielded from prosecution in jurisdictions with less robust police partnerships.

Nonetheless, turf battles between criminals continue to exist. These disputes are often seen in areas where gangs and other criminal networks are involved in trafficking and distributing illicit drugs. Researchers in Camden, NJ, studied violent crime near street corners with the presence of gangs (involved in drug distribution). Results of their research indicated that street corners with the presence of more than one gang have significantly more crime than those street corners with the presence of only one gang.[102] The scholars noted that these results are consistent with qualitative research suggesting that violence is likely in areas where territory is disputed.

Take, for example, the escalating drug trafficking-related violence in Mexico. Much of the violence had been a result of clashes between the drug trafficking organizations (DTOs) over territory within Mexico and key smuggling routes into the United States.[103] According to Mexican government official estimates, this violence has resulted in more than 34,500 deaths in Mexico since President Felipe Calderón took office in December 2006.[104] Targets of this violence most often include rival DTOs or affiliated gang members.[105] Increased violence and visibility of these battles have helped garner increased attention from both the Mexican and U.S. governments, which have, in turn, elevated their determination and resources to combat the DTOs.[106]

---

[101] U.S. Department of Justice, National Drug Intelligence Center, *National Drug Threat Assessment 2010,* Product No. 2010-Q0317-001, February 2010, pp. 12-13, http://www.justice.gov/ndic/pubs38/38661/38661p.pdf.

[102] Jerry H. Ratcliffe and Travis A. Taniguchi, "Is Crime Higher Around Drug Gang Street corners? Two Spatial Approaches to the Relationship Between Gang Set Spaces and Local Crime Levels," *Crime Patterns and Analysis*, vol. 1, no. 1 (2008), pp. 23 - 45.

[103] Some of the violence is also directed at the Mexican government, police, and military attempting to enforce the drug laws in Mexico. For more information on the violence, see CRS Report R41576, *Mexico's Drug Trafficking Organizations: Source and Scope of the Rising Violence*, by June S. Beittel.

[104] Viridiana Ríos and David A. Shirk, *Drug Violence In Mexico, Data and Analysis Through 2010*, University of San Diego, Trans-Border Institute, February 2011, http://justiceinmexico files.wordpress.com/2011/02/2011-tbi-drugviolence4.pdf.

[105] Targets have also included Mexican police, military, and government officials; journalists; and civilians—including Americans.

[106] For more information on U.S. and Mexican efforts to combat the DTOs, see CRS Report R41349, *U.S.-Mexican Security Cooperation: The Mérida Initiative and Beyond* , by Clare Ribando Seelke and Kristin M. Finklea.

Another way in which turf can be a barrier to criminals is that a heavy focus on turf can stunt criminals' profit if their activities are relegated to a particular turf. Focusing on a specific crime in a specific location may not prove to be the most profitable of business practices for criminals. Gangs, as mentioned, are notorious for violently defending the space in which they operate and controlling the activities that take place within given turf boundaries. While this has been standard practice, criminal gangs have modified this standard to expand their profitable activities both within and beyond their turf. According to the DEA, many "[g]angs have evolved from turf-oriented entities to profit-driven, organized criminal enterprises whose activities include not only retail drug distribution but also other aspects of the trade, including smuggling, transportation, and wholesale distribution."[107]

Evolution of Criminal Turf

As discussed, to date, turf may have been more readily established in the physical world than in the cyber world—at least by criminals. Some have predicted, however, that this landscape may change in the coming years. In the cyber world, the evolution of operating systems may provide a wider variety of turf platforms on which criminals may operate. The number of Windows-alternative operating systems is increasing, and malicious code that some criminals use to compromise Windows, for instance, may not be compatible across operating systems. This diversification may contribute to establishing various platforms of cyber turf on which differing cyber gangs and criminal organizations may specialize their operations. This may contribute to what some have predicted—possible turf wars between hackers and groups of hackers.[108]

Law Enforcement and Operational Turf

Just as territorial control impacts criminals, turf also influences law enforcement operations. While some crimes are investigated under the jurisdiction of a proprietary agency (e.g., the FBI is the lead federal agency responsible for terrorism investigations), other crimes are not investigated under such clear lines. For instance, various federal agencies, including the FBI, USSS, U.S. Postal Inspection Service (USPIS), and ICE are involved in investigating identity theft.[109] Multiple agencies investigating a particular genre of crime can open the doors to investigative overlaps (and possible turf battles) as well as data challenges. According to GAO, a "lack of coordination can lead to confusion, frustration, and a waste of law enforcement resources; pose a risk to law enforcement personnel; and limit the overall effectiveness of the federal effort."[110]

---

[107] U.S. Department of Justice, *FY2012 Performance Budget, Drug Enforcement Administration, U.S. Department of Justice, Congressional Budget Submission*, p. 11, http://www.justice.gov/jmd/2012justification/pdf/fy12-dea-justification.pdf.

[108] Kaspersky Lab presented a forecast for the 2011–2020 information technology (IT) landscape. Forecast details are discussed in "Cybercrime Outlook 2020 From Kaspersky Lab," *securelist.com*, February 11, 2011, http://www.securelist.com/en/analysis/204792165/Cybercrime_Outlook_2020_From_Kaspersky_Lab.

[109] For more information on identity theft investigations, see CRS Report R40599, *Identity Theft: Trends and Issues*, by Kristin M. Finklea. See also International Association of Chiefs of Police (IACP) National Law Enforcement Policy Center, *Identity Theft: Concepts and Issues Paper*, March 2002, p. 2, http://www.mrsc.org/artdocmisc/identity%20theft%20paper.pdf.

[110] U.S. Government Accountability Office, *Law Enforcement Coordination: DOJ Could Improve Its Process for Identifying Disagreements Among Agents*, GAO-11-314, April 2011, p. 2, http://www.gao.gov/new.items/d11314.pdf.

Investigative Overlaps

Jurisdictional battles between federal law enforcement agencies—particularly in areas of overlapping investigative authority—are not new phenomena. These battles have contributed, in part, to what some have characterized as inefficient information sharing. ATF's Project Gunrunner, for example, is one of various measures to reduce the illegal flow of weapons into Mexico. One purported cornerstone of Project Gunrunner is intelligence information sharing between federal, state, local, tribal, and international law enforcement partners.[111] It aims to disrupt the illegal flow of guns from the United States to Mexico, enhance U.S. and Mexican law enforcement coordination, and train U.S. and Mexican law enforcement officials to identify firearms traffickers. In November 2010, the DOJ Office of the Inspector General (OIG) issued a report on Project Gunrunner. The OIG report criticized Project Gunrunner, in part, because "ATF does not systematically and consistently exchange intelligence with its Mexican and some U.S. partner agencies."[112] These domestic partner agencies include DEA and ICE. This lack of information sharing, and subsequent criticism, exist despite the presence of a Memorandum of Understanding (MOU) between ATF and ICE agreeing to enhance information sharing in cases of shared jurisdiction. It is unclear, however, whether the criticized lack of coordination arose from jurisdictional conflicts between partner agencies or from inefficient project planning and outreach to policing partners. Regardless, Project Gunrunner's inadequacies highlight the difficulties of sharing investigative information across agencies.

Another example of shared jurisdiction and inter-agency competition involves the National Cyber Investigative Joint Task Force (NCIJTF). In 2008, the FBI established the NCIJTF to coordinate information from 18 intelligence and law enforcement agencies. This task force was created to share information on all domestic cyber threat investigations.[113] An April 2011 DOJ OIG report indicated that "the NCIJTF was not always sharing information about cyber threats among the partner agencies participating in the NCIJTF" and that "task force members first attempted to determine the relevancy and importance of its information to another agency's operations before sharing that information with another agency."[114] In essence, it appears that members were sharing information more on a need-to-know basis rather than automatically. In addition, the report indicated that during NCIJTF threat focus cell meetings, where agencies share new information regarding specific cyber threats, some agencies were asked to leave.

Recently, GAO released a study on law enforcement coordination within DOJ. Over one-third (37%) of DOJ agents from the FBI, DEA, ATF, and U.S. Marshals interviewed by GAO indicated that they had experienced disagreements with other DOJ agencies regarding roles and responsibilities in an investigation.[115] Further, of those agents reporting disagreements, 78%

---

[111] ATF, *Project Gunrunner*, http://www.atf.gov/firearms/programs/project-gunrunner/. For more information on Project Gunrunner, see CRS Report R41206, *The Bureau of Alcohol, Tobacco, Firearms and Explosives (ATF): Budget and Operations for FY2011*, by William J. Krouse.

[112] U.S. Department of Justice, Office of the Inspector General, Review of ATF's Project Gunrunner, I-2011-001, November 2010, p. iii, http://www.justice.gov/oig/reports/ATF/e1101.pdf.

[113] Federal Bureau of Investigation, *National Cyber Investigative Joint Task Force*, http://www.fbi.gov/about-us/investigate/cyber/ncijtf.

[114] U.S. Department of Justice, Office of the Inspector General, Audit Division, *The Federal Bureau of Investigation's Ability to Address the National Security Cyber Intrusion Threat*, Audit Report 11-22, April 2011, pp. iv - vii, http://www.justice.gov/oig/reports/FBI/a1122r.pdf.

[115] U.S. Government Accountability Office, *Law Enforcement Coordination: DOJ Could Improve Its Process for Identifying Disagreements Among Agents*, GAO-11-314, April 2011, p. 8, http://www.gao.gov/new.items/d11314.pdf.

---

indicated that these inter-agency disputes adversely impacted investigations. Also within the subset of agents reporting disagreements, 28% indicated that the source of the problem was a lack of information sharing from other agencies conducting similar investigations. The GAO study also suggests that the more agencies there are sharing jurisdiction on a particular investigative area, the less clear the agents may be regarding their agency's roles and responsibilities.[116] This lack of clarity may invite more turf battles and disputes that could in turn hamper an investigation.

Of note, not all investigative overlaps result in turf battles, and not all turf battles are ultimately detrimental to law enforcement efforts. Agencies can capitalize on shared jurisdiction and effectively pool their efforts, as is discussed in detail in the section "Interagency Cooperation and Information Sharing."

Information and Data Sharing

When multiple agencies investigate a particular type of crime, a lack of centralized, compatible, comprehensive data may hamper their abilities to measure the true scope of a crime, share information, and coordinate investigations.

For instance, several federal agencies investigate and record information on bulk cash smuggling. These include the DEA through the National Seizure System at the El Paso Intelligence Center (EPIC), ICE through its Bulk Cash Smuggling Center, and the Department of the Treasury through the Treasury Enforcement Communications System database. Each of these databases is distinct from the others, and they are not set up to automatically share information. Of note, the Office of National Drug Control Policy (ONDCP) has recommended that increased information sharing among federal agencies—as well as between federal, state, and local law enforcement—could aid in investigations of DTOs involved in bulk cash smuggling.[117]

Similarly, there are multiple agencies gathering information on cybercrime and specific subsets of cybercrime. For example, there are various agencies collecting data on identity theft. The FBI partners with the National White Collar Crime Center to host the Internet Crime Complaint Center (IC3). The IC3 has a database of cybercrime complaints, including those regarding identity theft. The Federal Trade Commission is another agency maintaining a database of consumer complaints on a range of frauds such as identity theft. ICE also collects this information through its Cyber Crime Center (C3), and the USPIS maintains information in its Financial Crimes Database. The range of agencies and databases hosting information on identity theft can present challenges to law enforcement effectively combating the crime. Moreover, the President's Identity Theft Task Force noted that

> One barrier to more complete coordination is that identity theft information resides in multiple databases, even within individual law enforcement agencies. A single instance of identity theft may result in information being posted at federal, state, and local law enforcement agencies, credit reporting agencies, credit issuers, financial institutions, telecommunications companies, and regulatory agencies. This, in turn, leads to the inefficient "stove-piping" of relevant data and intelligence. Additionally, in many cases, agencies do not

---

[116] Ibid., p. 10.

[117] Office of National Drug Control Strategy, *National Southwest Border Counternarcotics Strategy*, June 2009, p. 25.

or cannot share information with other agencies, making it difficult to determine whether an identity theft complaint is related to a single incident or a series of incidents.[118]

Even when centralized databases, information sharing mechanisms, or directives are available, inter-agency coordination and sharing may not occur. For instance, DOJ has issued two MOUs in an attempt to clarify FBI and ATF roles in explosives investigations.[119] The first MOU, in 2004, reportedly had ambiguous language regarding how to determine a lead agency in explosives investigations. In addition, DOJ, FBI, and ATF did not implement the outlined procedures regarding information sharing, database consolidation, training, and laboratory resources.[120] A subsequent 2008 MOU reportedly had similar issues in that it did not clarify investigative jurisdiction.[121] DOJ's Office of the Inspector General (OIG) has indicated that despite two MOUs, FBI and ATF do not adequately coordinate their explosives investigations and continue to dispute which is the lead agency in a given investigation.[122] Further, as of 2009, the two agencies continued to maintain separate explosives-related databases despite instructions in the 2004 MOU directing their consolidation.[123]

Jurisdictional battles impacting information sharing are not exclusive to federal law enforcement agencies. Such discrepancies may exist between federal and state or local law enforcement, as well as between federal law enforcement and foreign counterparts. For example, multilateral information relating to drug, alien, and weapon smuggling is intended to be shared through EPIC.[124] EPIC is a fully coordinated, multi-agency tactical intelligence center supported by databases and resources from member agencies. Its online query capability consists of 33 federal databases, 6 commercial databases, and its own internal database. It operates a 24/7 watch program manned by special agents, investigative assistants, and intelligence analysts to provide timely tactical intelligence in support of field operations. In a June 2010 review of the El Paso Intelligence Center, DOJ's OIG indicated that the lack of an up-to-date agreement between EPIC and its member agencies has led to several coordination issues, including a lack of information sharing among agencies.[125]

---

[118] The President's Identity Theft Task Force, *Combating Identity Theft: A Strategic Plan*, April 23, 2007, p. 55, http://www.identitytheft.gov/reports/StrategicPlan.pdf.

[119] U.S. Department of Justice, Office of the Inspector General, *Explosives Investigation Coordination Between the Federal Bureau of Investigation and the Bureau of Alcohol, Tobacco, Firearms and Explosives*, Audit Report 10-01, October 2009, see Appendix IV and Appendix VI, http://www.justice.gov/oig/reports/plus/a1001.pdf.

[120] Ibid., p. ii.

[121] Ibid., p. iii.

[122] Ibid., p. ii.

[123] GAO has subsequently noted DOJ plans to implement an information sharing system between the FBI and ATF. U.S. Government Accountability Office, *Opportunities to Reduce Potential Duplication in Government Programs*, GAO-11-318SP, March 2011, http://www.gao.gov/ereport/GAO-11-318SP/data_center/Homeland_security— Law_enforcement/The_Department_of_Justice_plans_actions_to_reduce_overlap_in_explosives_investigations,_but_ monitoring_is_needed_to_ensure_successful_implementation#_ftnref4.

[124] Agencies represented at EPIC include DEA (which leads the center), CBP, ICE, U.S. Coast Guard, USSS, Department of Defense (DOD), Department of the Interior, FBI, ATF, U.S. Marshals Service, Federal Aviation Administration, National Drug Intelligence Center (NDIC), Internal Revenue Service, National Geospatial-Intelligence Agency, Joint Task Force-North, Joint Interagency Task Force-South, Texas Department of Public Safety, Texas Air National Guard, and the El Paso County Sheriff's Office. For more information on EPIC, see http://www.justice.gov/ dea/programs/epic.htm.

[125] U.S. Department of Justice, Office of the Inspector General, *Review of the Drug Enforcement Administration's El Paso Intelligence Center*, I-2010-005, June 2010, p. ii, http://www.justice.gov/oig/reports/DEA/a1005.pdf.

Similar OIG critiques have been made of the National Gang Intelligence Center (NGIC). The NGIC coordinates intelligence information from federal, state, and local policing agencies. It supports law enforcement investigations by providing strategic and tactical analysis of intelligence.[126] In a November 2009 DOJ OIG review of DOJ's anti-gang intelligence and coordination centers (including NGIC), the OIG concluded that the NGIC had not created a gang information database, as had been directed by Congress.[127] Further, the "NGIC is perceived as predominately an FBI organization, and it has not developed the capability to effectively share gang intelligence and information with other law enforcement organizations." It cannot be determined however, whether the coordination flaws were due to jurisdictional struggles between partner agencies or to a lack of information-sharing mechanisms in place.

When exercising its oversight role, one issue Congress may wish to explore is whether existing MOUs and other inter-agency agreements regarding information sharing are being adequately formulated and implemented. Congress may also investigate the extent to which these agreements are being effectively overseen by applicable agency leadership.

U.S. Law Enforcement Efforts to Overcome Barriers

Modern-day criminals take advantage of geographic borders, criminal turf, cyberspace, and law enforcement jurisdictions. This has led law enforcement to transform their crime fighting efforts. For instance, the FBI has—particularly since September 11, 2001—relied more heavily on collaboration, information sharing, and technology.[128] The following sections outline how federal law enforcement has relied on interagency cooperation and technological implementation to confront 21st century crime.

Interagency Cooperation and Information Sharing

As discussed, crimes—particularly those considered cybercrimes or that contain a cyber component—are increasingly trans-border and transnational. Further, criminal organizations are becoming less hierarchical and more networked in structure. These evolutions in the nature of crime and criminal organizations may require that law enforcement simultaneously become more nimble and networked in order to effectively counter the threats. Generally, law enforcement agencies and government entities charged with combating criminal networks are relatively hierarchical in comparison, and some experts have suggested that "hierarchies have a difficult time fighting networks."[129] This does not necessarily mean that it would be possible or even beneficial to make law enforcement and government entities less hierarchical. However, law

---

[126] For more information on the NGIC, see http://www.fbi.gov/about-us/investigate/vc_majorthefts/gangs/ngic.

[127] U.S. Department of Justice, Office of the Inspector General, *A Review of the Department's Anti-Gang Intelligence and Coordination Centers*, I-2010-001, November 2009, http://www.justice.gov/oig/reports/FBI/i2010001.pdf.

[128] Federal Bureau of Investigation, "Richard A. McFeely, Special Agent in Charge, FBI, Statement Before the Senate Judiciary Committee, Wilmington, Delaware," June 20, 2011, http://www.fbi.gov/news/testimony/information-sharing-efforts-with-partners-span-many-fbi-programs.

[129] "The Advent of Netwar (Revisited)," in *Networks and Netwars: The Future of Terror, Crime, and Militancy*, ed. John Arquilla and David Ronfeldt, p. 15.

enforcement adoption of networked practices (rather than actual structure) may better equip them to confront 21st century criminals.[130]

One such networked practice involves interagency coordination. Federal law enforcement has already taken steps to network with other federal, state, local, and international partners. This model has been used for decades to combat more traditional crime, and it has more recently been used to combat cybercrime. For instance, the FBI began embedding agents with international law enforcement partners in Romania in 2006 in order to target cyber criminals.[131] FBI collaboration has since been expanded to countries including Estonia, Ukraine, and the Netherlands.[132] These partnerships have proved beneficial in investigating and prosecuting transnational criminals. For example, law enforcement agencies including the FBI, USSS, Estonian Central Criminal Police, Netherlands Police Agency National Crime Squad High Tech Crime Unit, and the Netherlands National Public Prosecutor's Office, as well as the Hong Kong Police Force, all contributed to investigating a criminal network involved in hacking the RBS WorldPay computer network.[133] Five hackers have been indicted in the case. These individuals allegedly defeated the encryption used by RBS WorldPay to protect customer information associated with the payroll card processing system. Using counterfeit payroll debit cards—cards that allow employees to withdraw their regular salaries from ATMs—the hackers and their associates withdrew more than $9 million from over 2,100 ATMs across at least 280 cities around the globe—including in the United States, Russia, Ukraine, Estonia, Italy, Hong Kong, Japan, and Canada. Notably, the over $9 million loss occurred in under 12 hours.[134] In August 2010, Estonia extradited to the United States one of the principal leaders of the hacking ring, who has since been arraigned on charges of conspiracy to commit wire fraud, wire fraud, conspiracy to commit computer fraud, computer fraud, and aggravated identity theft.[135]

In another case, from June 2011, U.S., Colombian, and Italian law enforcement worked together to investigate "La Oficina de Envigado," a Colombian narcotics trafficking and money laundering network.[136] The organization—a vestige of the notorious Medellín Cartel—is based in Medellín, Colombia, but operates internationally, including in Massachusetts. Authorities seized 48 bank accounts in the United States. In addition, officials estimate that through the course of this operation, known as "Operation Fire and Ice," they seized over $200 million in cash, over 1,100 kilograms of cocaine, and 46 kilograms of heroin around the world.[137]

---

[130] Ibid., p. 18.

[131] Robert McMillan, "FBI Embeds Cyber-Investigators in Ukraine, Estonia," *PCWorld*, March 4, 2010, http://www.pcworld.com/article/190837/fbi_embeds_cyberinvestigators_in_ukraine_estonia.html. Embedding agents with international law enforcement partners allows U.S. and foreign law enforcement to work together (in the same location) to counter specific threats.

[132] Ibid.

[133] RBS WorldPay is an Atlanta, GA-based credit card processing company that is part of the Royal Bank of Scotland. For more information on this case, see U.S. Department of Justice, "Alleged International Hacking Ring Caught in $9 Million Fraud," press release, November 10, 2009, http://www.justice.gov/opa/pr/2009/November/09-crm-1212.html.

[134] Ibid.

[135] U.S. Department of Justice, "International Hacker Arraigned After Extradition," press release, August 6, 2010, http://www.justice.gov/usao/gan/press/2010/08-06-10.pdf.

[136] For more information, see Drug Enforcement Administration, "Twenty Alleged Members and Associates of Colombia's Largest Drug Cartel Charged," press release, June 2, 2011, http://www.justice.gov/dea/pubs/states/newsrel/2011/boston060211.html.

[137] "Drug money laundering ring with ties to Colombia and Italy busted in Boston," *The Boston Globe*, June 2, 2011, http://www.boston.com/news/local/breaking_news/2011/06/multi-million_m.html.

Federal law enforcement agencies may work with one another (and with their international counterparts), either informally or through formal agreements, to counter the transnational nature of crimes—both traditional and cyber. For example, the United States is a signatory to the United Nations Convention Against Transnational Organized Crime as well as the Council of Europe's Convention on Cybercrime and participates in the Group of 8 (G8)[138] High Tech Crime Subgroup, as discussed below.

United Nations Convention Against Transnational Organized Crime

The United Nations Convention Against Transnational Organized Crime is the primary international tool for combating organized crime.[139] In 2005, the United States ratified the convention as well as the companion protocols on trafficking in persons and smuggling of migrants. Among other provisions, the convention provides for greater law enforcement cooperation and mutual legal assistance across nations where there were no previous agreements for such assistance. The convention also requires signatories to criminalize certain offenses such as participation in an organized criminal group, money laundering, corruption, and obstruction of justice. It also requires the enhancement of training and technical assistance to combat transnational organized crime. By ratifying the convention in 2005, Congress took a step in working with foreign governments and law enforcement agencies to combat multi-national and multi-jurisdictional organized crime. Given the increasingly transnational nature of organized crime, this coordination with international organizations is seen as essential.[140]

Council of Europe Convention on Cybercrime

The Council of Europe's Convention on Cybercrime was developed in 2001 to address several categories of crimes committed via the internet and other information networks.[141] It is the first international treaty on this issue, and its primary goal is to "pursue a common criminal policy aimed at the protection of society against cybercrime, especially by adopting appropriate legislation and fostering international co-operation." To date, 47 countries are signatories to the convention and 31 of these—including the United States—have ratified it.[142]

As mentioned, not all activities considered to be crimes in one country are also considered criminal acts in another. Further, there is not a harmonized view on what constitutes cyber or computer-related crime. Signatories to the convention, however, must define criminal offenses

---

[138] The G8 was established in 1975 as a forum for world leaders to discuss economic issues. It has since expanded to include subgroups, one of which focuses on high tech crime.

[139] United Nations Office of Drugs and Crime, *United Nations Convention Against Transnational Organized Crime and the Protocols Thereto*, United Nations, New York, 2004.

[140] From remarks by Bruce Swartz, Deputy Assistant Attorney General, Criminal Division, U.S. Department of Justice, at U.S. Congress, Senate Committee on Foreign Relations, *Hearing on Law Enforcement Treaties: Treaty Doc. 107-18, Inter-American Convention Against Terrorism; Treaty Doc. 108-6, Protocol of Amendment to the International Convention on the Simplification and Harmonization of Customs Procedures; Treaty Doc. 108-11, Council of Europe Convention on Cybercrime; Treaty Doc. 108-16, U.N. Convention Against Transnational Organized Crime and Protocols on Trafficking in Persons and Smuggling of Migrants*, 108th Cong., 2nd sess., June 17, 2004, pp. 29-37.

[141] For more information on the Convention, see archived CRS Report RS21208, *Cybercrime: The Council of Europe Convention*, by Kristin Archick. A copy of the Convention is available at http://conventions.coe.int/Treaty/EN/Treaties/html/185.htm.

[142] The U.S. Senate ratified the Convention on August 3, 2006. For the current list of signatories and ratifications, see http://conventions.coe.int/Treaty/Commun/ChercheSig.asp?NT=185&CM=1&DF=&CL=ENG.

---

and sanctions under their domestic laws for four categories of computer-related crimes: security breaches such as hacking, illegal data interception, and system interferences that compromise network integrity and availability; fraud and forgery; child pornography; and copyright infringements. The convention also requires signatories to establish domestic procedures for detecting, investigating, and prosecuting computer crimes, as well as collecting electronic evidence of any criminal offense. It also requires that signatories engage in international cooperation "to the widest extent possible."

G8 High Tech Crime Subgroup

DOJ is a key player in U.S. participation in the G8 Subgroup on High Tech Crime. In 1996, the G8 created the Lyon group of experts on transnational organized crime. These experts developed Forty Recommendations to combat transnational organized crime. Subsequently, the G8 created various subgroups (one of which is a High Tech Crime subgroup) to address various crime-related issues.[143] The subgroup has created a Network for 24-Hour Points of Contact for high tech crime. It has negotiated an action plan and a set of widely accepted principles to combat high tech crime. It has also created numerous best practices documents such as guides for securing computer networks, requesting international assistance, drafting legislation, and tracing networked communications across borders. The subgroup has assessed threats and the impact on law enforcement from new technology such as encryption as well as malicious internet activities such as viruses and worms. It has also sponsored training conferences for cybercrime agencies as well as conferences for law enforcement and industry on improved cooperation.[144]

Interagency Agreements

One mechanism that federal law enforcement agencies have used to try to minimize jurisdictional discrepancies and coordinate work is through interagency agreements and Memoranda of Understanding (MOUs). For instance, on June 30, 2009, ATF and ICE signed an MOU, citing a shared jurisdiction in combating criminal organizations engaging in violent crime and drug trafficking. The agencies agreed to involve one another in cases of shared jurisdiction and to enhance information sharing in such cases.[145] The DOJ OIG found that, despite this MOU,

> ATF and ICE do not work together effectively on investigations of firearms trafficking to Mexico, and therefore ATF's Project Gunrunner cases do not benefit from ICE's intelligence and prosecutorial options. ATF and ICE rarely conduct joint investigations of firearms trafficking to Mexico, do not consistently notify each other of their firearms trafficking cases, and do not consistently coordinate their investigative work with each other.[146]

---

[143] U.S. Department of Justice, *Background on the G8*, http://www.justice.gov/criminal/cybercrime/g82004/ g8_background.html.

[144] Ibid.

[145] Statement of Janice Ayala, Deputy Assistant Director, Office of Investigations, U.S. Immigration and Customs Enforcement, Department of Homeland Security, before the U.S. Congress, House Committee on Homeland Security, Subcommittee on Border, Maritime, and Global Counterterrorism, *Cargo Security at Land Ports of Entry: Are We Meeting the Challenge?*, 111th Cong., 1st sess., October 22, 2009.

[146] U.S. Department of Justice, Office of the Inspector General, Review of ATF's Project Gunrunner, I-2011-001, November 2010, p. vi, http://www.justice.gov/oig/reports/ATF/e1101.pdf.

The OIG attributed this lack of information sharing to both an unawareness of the MOU's existence as well as misunderstanding of its purpose.

ICE also shares an interagency cooperation agreement with the DEA that has been in effect since June 18, 2009. The agencies agree to share information through the DEA's Special Operations Division, the Organized Crime Drug Enforcement Task Force (OCDETF) program Fusion Center, and EPIC. The agreement also allows ICE to select agents for cross-designation by the DEA Administrator and permits these ICE agents to investigate narcotics smuggling with a clear nexus to the U.S. border. It also provides procedures for deconfliction[147] and operational coordination in domestic and international cases.[148] On August 10, 2009, ICE and DOJ signed two MOUs to enhance information sharing at the OCDETF Fusion Center and the International Organized Crime Intelligence and Operations Center (IOC-2).[149] It is unknown, however, how well the agreements and MOUs between ICE and DEA as well as between ICE and DOJ have reduced any turf battles in their areas of overlapping jurisdiction.

Fusion Centers and Task Forces

As modern law enforcement operations have become increasingly intelligence-led, agencies have come to rely heavily on fusion centers and task forces. According to DHS, fusion centers and task forces (with specific reference to Joint Terrorism Task Forces, or JTTFs) serve "distinct, but complementary roles."[150] Fusion centers have been defined as a "collaborative effort of two or more Federal, state, local, or tribal government agencies that combines resources, expertise, or information with the goal of maximizing the ability of such agencies to detect, prevent, investigate, apprehend, and respond to criminal or terrorist activity."[151] DHS has indicated that

> [F]usion centers serve as focal points within the state and local environment for the receipt, analysis, gathering, and sharing of threat-related information among federal and state, local, tribal, and territorial (SLTT) partners. They produce actionable intelligence for dissemination, which can aid other law enforcement organizations, including the JTTFs, in their investigative operations.[152]

While fusion centers are generally intelligence-based, law enforcement task forces appear to be generally operational in nature.[153] These multi-jurisdictional entities are established to counter a

---

[147] According to DOJ, deconfliction means "ensure[ing] that two or more agencies are not duplicating resources or that one agency's investigation will not have a negative impact on another agency's investigation." In other words, deconfliction is intended, in part, to reduce turf battles. See U.S. Department of Justice, "ICE and DOJ Sign Agreements to Share Information on Drug Trafficking and Organized Crime," press release, August 10, 2009, http://www.justice.gov/opa/pr/2009/August/09-crm-784.html.

[148] Statement of Janice Ayala, Deputy Assistant Director, Office of Investigations, U.S. Immigration and Customs Enforcement, Department of Homeland Security, before the U.S. Congress, House Committee on Homeland Security, Subcommittee on Border, Maritime, and Global Counterterrorism, *Cargo Security at Land Ports of Entry: Are We Meeting the Challenge?*, 111th Cong., 1st sess., October 22, 2009.

[149] U.S. Department of Justice, "ICE and DOJ Sign Agreements to Share Information on Drug Trafficking and Organized Crime," press release, August 10, 2009, http://www.justice.gov/opa/pr/2009/August/09-crm-784.html.

[150] Department of Homeland Security, *Fusion Centers and Joint Terrorism Task Forces*, February 28, 2011, http://www.dhs.gov/files/programs/gc_1298911926746.shtm.

[151] P.L. 110-53, Aug. 3, 2007, §511, 121 STAT. 322. Amends *Homeland Security Act of 2002* by adding §210A(j).

[152] Department of Homeland Security, *Fusion Centers and Joint Terrorism Task Forces*, February 28, 2011, http://www.dhs.gov/files/programs/gc_1298911926746.shtm.

[153] There are some entities that are hybrid centers, focusing both on intelligence and operations. The National Counter (continued...)

---

specific threat such as violent gangs[154] or online fraud.[155] The sections below discuss selected fusion centers and task forces.

Fusion Center Model

The majority of fusion centers, located in states and major urban areas throughout the country, were created post-9/11, though interagency information sharing centers had been emerging since at least the 1990s.[156] One precursor to the formal fusion center concept is the High Intensity Drug Trafficking Area (HIDTA) program. The HIDTA program, originally authorized by the Anti-Drug Abuse Act of 1988 (P.L. 100-690),[157] provides assistance to federal, state, and local law enforcement operating in areas deemed as the most impacted by drug trafficking. Each HIDTA is governed by a separate executive board comprised of about eight federal agencies and eight state or local agencies. The program's main goals are to

- assess regional drug threats;

- develop strategies focusing efforts on combating drug trafficking threats;

- create and fund initiatives to improve these strategies;

- facilitate coordination between federal, state, and local efforts; and

- produce efficient drug control efforts to reduce/eliminate the impact of drug trafficking.[158]

The Director of the Office of National Drug Control Policy (ONDCP) has the authority to designate areas within the United States and its territories that are centers of illegal drug production, manufacturing, importation, or distribution as HIDTAs—of which there are currently 28.[159] The Southwest Border Region HIDTA, for example, includes portions of California, Arizona, New Mexico, and Texas. The HIDTA collects and shares intelligence and coordinates task forces composed of federal, state, and local agencies that target drug-trafficking operations along the border. In one case from June 2011, the Milwaukee, WI, HIDTA was involved in the

---

(...continued)

Terrorism Center (NCTC), for example, is a center for joint intelligence and operational planning. Similarly, the National Intellectual Property Rights Coordination Center (IPR Center) serves as an information repository as well as a place to develop initiatives and coordinate law enforcement investigations.

[154] The FBI leads 160 Violent Gang Safe Streets Task Forces around the country. For more information, see http://www.fbi.gov/about-us/investigate/vc_majorthefts/gangs/violent-gangs-task-forces.

[155] The USSS leads 28 Electronic Fraud Task Forces. Information provided to CRS by USSS Congressional Affairs. For more information, see http://www.secretservice.gov/ectf.shtml.

[156] For more information on fusion centers, see archived CRS Report RL34070, *Fusion Centers: Issues and Options for Congress*, by John Rollins.

[157] 21 U.S.C. §1706.

[158] Office of National Drug Control Policy, The High-Intensity Drug Trafficking Area Program: An Overview, http://whitehousedrugpolicy.gov/hidta/overview.html.

[159] Ibid. Four main criteria are considered when designating an area as a HIDTA: "(1) the extent to which the area is a significant center of illegal drug production, manufacturing, importation, or distribution; (2) the extent to which State, local, and tribal law enforcement agencies have committed resources to respond to the drug trafficking problem in the area, thereby indicating a determination to respond aggressively to the problem; (3) the extent to which drug-related activities in the area are having a significant harmful impact in the area, and in other areas of the country; and (4) the extent to which a significant increase in allocation of Federal resources is necessary to respond adequately to drug related activities in the area."

---

indictments of 24 individuals involved in a drug trafficking and illegal gambling ring. Couriers in the network transported hundreds of pounds of marijuana from Seattle, WA, and Vancouver, BC, to Minnesota, Wisconsin, and Illinois, and transported bulk cash—about $1.3 million in proceeds from drug sales and illegal gambling—back to the Pacific Northwest.[160]

Several law enforcement fusion centers have been created to target criminal networks, including the Organized Crime Drug Enforcement Task Force (OCDETF) Fusion Center (OFC), the International Organized Crime Intelligence and Operations Center (IOC-2), the National Gang Intelligence Center (NGIC), and the El Paso Intelligence Center (EPIC). They are charged with consolidating and disseminating intelligence on various organized crime matters. For instance, the OFC assimilates information for the OCDETF Program, targeting major drug trafficking and money laundering organizations. The IOC-2—housed at the OFC—was created by DOJ in 2009 to bring together the FBI; ICE; DEA; IRS; ATF; USSS; USPIS; U.S. Department of State, Bureau of Diplomatic Security; U.S. Department of Labor, Office of the Inspector General; and DOJ's Criminal Division in partnership with the 94 U.S. Attorneys' Offices and the U.S. Department of the Treasury, Office of Terrorism and Financial Intelligence. The IOC-2 is charged with analyzing and resolving information conflicts on a host of organized crime cases, not solely those that center on drug trafficking.

Despite successes using the fusion center model, not all fusion centers have been funded. While NGIC, EPIC, and the OFC have received funding, the IOC-2 has not. One issue that Congress may consider is whether such intelligence-sharing centers bolster federal law enforcement's abilities to combat networked, trans-border crime. If they are effective, Congress may debate whether increasing resources for existing centers would in turn increase law enforcement operations. Increased funding could boost law enforcement investigations in number and/or in quality. One question surrounding any increase in funding for investigations is whether enhanced investigative resources are balanced with complementary resources for prosecutions. If policy makers enable law enforcement to investigate a greater number of cases, they may chose to consider whether they are balancing investigative resources with prosecutorial resources.

With respect to the coordination of federal efforts to combat criminal networks, one non-legislative option that Congress may consider is enforcing its oversight over existing fusion centers. As mentioned, in June 2010, the DOJ Office of the Inspector General (OIG) issued a review of EPIC. The review suggested that, while EPIC's users value its products, EPIC could gain from fully developing the National Seizure System and coordinating the HIDTA program, consistently coordinating with intelligence organizations across the country, maintaining and analyzing current information from all available sources, and creating objective performance measures by which to evaluate its programs, among other things.[161] Before determining whether to increase, decrease, or maintain funding for existing fusion centers, policy makers may debate whether these centers have taken measures to most effectively obtain their respective goals. For instance, has EPIC taken measures to analyze current information from all its available resources or has the OFC effectively used its resources to pursue CPOT targets?

---

[160] U.S. Department of Justice, "Twenty-Four Defendants Federally Indicted in Southeast Wisconsin Drug Trafficking and Illegal Gambling Case," press release, June 2, 2011, http://www.justice.gov/usao/wie/press_releases/2011/pr20110602_24_Defendants_Indicted_Drug_Trafficking-Illegal_Gambling.pdf.

[161] U.S. Department of Justice, Office of the Inspector General, *Review of the Drug Enforcement Administration's El Paso Intelligence Center*, I-2010-005, June 2010, p. ii, http://www.justice.gov/oig/reports/DEA/a1005.pdf.

Task Force Model

Federal law enforcement has increasingly relied on the task force model to coordinate investigations. One such task force is the Organized Crime Drug Enforcement Task Force (OCDETF) program. The OCDETF program targets—with the intent to disrupt and dismantle—major drug trafficking and money laundering organizations. Federal agencies that participate in the OCDETF Program include the DEA, FBI, ICE, ATF, U.S. Marshals, Internal Revenue Service (IRS), U.S. Coast Guard (USCG), the 94 U.S. Attorneys Offices (USAOs), and DOJ's Criminal and Tax Divisions. These federal agencies also collaborate with state and local law enforcement. The OCDETFs operate in nine regions around the country and target those organizations that have been identified on the Consolidated Priority Organization Targets (CPOT) List, which is the "most wanted" list for leaders of drug trafficking and money laundering organizations.[162] In FY2010, OCDETF filed 2,783 cases with the U.S. Attorneys Offices.[163]

While OCDETFs operate throughout the country, Border Enforcement Security Taskforces (BESTs) operate along the northern and southern borders. The BEST initiative consists of a series of multi-agency investigative task forces, of which ICE is the lead agency.[164] They seek to identify, disrupt, and dismantle criminal organizations posing significant threats to border security along both borders. Other agency participants include CBP, DEA, ATF, FBI, USCG, and the U.S. Attorneys Offices, and state and local law enforcement. The Mexican law enforcement agency Secretaria de Seguridad Publica is a partner along the Southwest border. On the northern border, Canadian law enforcement agencies like the Canada Border Services Agency, the Royal Canadian Mounted Police, the Ontario Provincial Police, the Niagara Regional Police Service, the Toronto Metropolitan Police, the Windsor Police Service, and the Amherstburg Police Service are active members. The Argentinean customs agency is part of the Miami BEST and the Colombian National Police is part of both the Miami and New York-New Jersey BESTs. Currently, there are 21 BESTs with locations around the United States and in Mexico. Each BEST concentrates on the prevalent threats in its area. On the southern border, for instance, this entails cross-border violence, weapons smuggling and trafficking, illegal drug and other contraband smuggling, money laundering and bulk cash smuggling, as well as human smuggling and trafficking.

Both policy makers and Administration officials have been concerned about financial fraud, particularly as the nation emerges from the most recent economic downturn. Because of these concerns, President Obama established a Financial Fraud Enforcement Task Force in November 2009.[165] The task force, chaired by the Attorney General, includes more than 20 federal agencies, the U.S. Attorneys Offices, and state and local partners. It targets a range of financial crimes from mortgage fraud and identity theft to credit card fraud and Ponzi schemes. Recently, the task force was involved in investigating and prosecuting a husband and wife team for defrauding over 250 individuals of about $1.5 million through an internet fraud scheme. The couple advertised high-end kitchen appliances on e-Bay, though they were not licensed dealers of these products. When

---

[162] U.S. Department of Justice, *FY2012 Budget and Performance Summary*, Interagency Crime and Drug Enforcement (ICDE), http://www.justice.gov/jmd/2012summary/pdf/fy12-icde-bud-summary.pdf.

[163] Data provided to CRS by USAO Congressional Affairs.

[164] Department of Homeland Security, U.S. Immigration and Customs Enforcement (ICE), *Fact Sheet:* Border Enforcement Security Task Forces, August 2010, http://www.ice.gov/news/library/factsheets/best.htm.

[165] For more information, see http://www.stopfraud.gov/.

customers bought the advertised items, the team of perpetrators used this money to purchase luxury items and stocks and did not to deliver the merchandise.[166]

One task force centered around cyber threats is the National Cyber Investigative Joint Task Force (NCIJTF), led by the FBI. The NCIJTF includes 18 law enforcement and intelligence agencies that work together to counter a variety of cyber threats, including national security intrusions, criminal intrusions, online child pornography, intellectual property rights violations, and internet fraud.[167] Within this task force model, the FBI operates smaller Threat Focus Cells that center around specific types of cyber threat such as botnets.[168] The Botnet Focus Cell was instrumental in countering the Mariposa botnet. This botnet, also known as "Butterfly Bot," was an information-stealing botnet that infected up to 12 million computers around the world. Butterfly Bot stole passwords for websites and financial institutions as well as credit card and bank account information from computer users. The FBI investigated this case in collaboration with Spanish and Slovenian police, who arrested both users and the creator of the botnet.[169]

Policy makers may choose to evaluate whether the task force model is an effective means to share information and counter emerging threats. As illustrated, turf battles, even between agencies that have established working relationships, can hinder investigations. Agencies may be at odds over leadership in a given case. They may also share information on a "need to know" rather than a "need to share" basis.[170] Carefully protecting information, however, is not inherently problematic. The more people who have access to information, the greater the chances it can be leaked or intercepted by malicious actors. The need to keep investigative information from criminals' eyes is an incentive to keep intelligence information among as few individuals as possible.[171] Nonetheless, Congress may debate the appropriate level of information sharing within task forces as well as through other inter-agency forums.

Information Sharing Systems

In addition to the benefits of operational collaboration and coordination, policy makers and law enforcement have cited the value of interagency information sharing. The push for information sharing has been more visible regarding the investigation of terrorism and related crimes than it

---

[166] Federal Bureau of Investigation, "E-Bay Fraudster Sentenced to 12½ Years in Prison ," press release, May 31, 2011, http://www.fbi.gov/lasvegas/press-releases/2011/e-bay-fraudster-sentenced-to-12-1-2-years-in-prison.

[167] U.S. Department of Justice, Office of the Inspector General, Audit Division, *The Federal Bureau of Investigation's Ability to Address the National Security Cyber Intrusion Threat*, Audit Report 11-22, April 2011, pp. ii - iii, http://www.justice.gov/oig/reports/FBI/a1122r.pdf. See also Federal Bureau of Investigation, *National Cyber Investigative Joint Task Force*, http://www fbi.gov/about-us/investigate/cyber/ncijtf.

[168] See remarks of Robert S. Mueller, III, Director, Federal Bureau of Investigation, "International Conference on Cyber Security 2010," August 5, 2010, http://www.fbi.gov/news/speeches/using-partnerships-to-combat-cyber-threats.

[169] Federal Bureau of Investigation, "FBI, Slovenian and Spanish Police Arrest Mariposa Botnet Creator, Operators," press release, July 28, 2010, http://www fbi.gov/news/pressrel/press-releases/fbi-slovenian-and-spanish-police-arrest-mariposa-botnet-creator-operators.

[170] The continuum between need to know and need to share has most often been discussed in the arena of counterterrorism intelligence information sharing. See, for instance, U.S. Congress, House Committee on Government Reform, *Moving From "Need to Know" to Need to Share": A Review of the 9/11 Commission's Recommendations*, 108th Cong., 2nd sess., August 3, 2004.

[171] Michael E. Buerger, Karen E. Gardner, and Bernard H. Levin, et al., *Incorporating Local Police Agencies Into a National Intelligence Network*, Futures Working Group, Futures Working Group White Paper Series, Vol. 1, No. 1, July 2008, pp. 42-43, http://fwg.cos.ucf.edu/publications/LocalIntel.pdf.

has been for the investigation of more traditional crime. For instance, in the 2004 Intelligence Reform and Terrorism Prevention Act (P.L. 108-458), Congress mandated the creation of an Information Sharing Environment—commonly known as the "ISE."[172] Through this act, Congress also directed that the ISE provide and facilitate the means of sharing terrorism information among all appropriate federal, state, local, and tribal entities as well as the private sector through the use of policy guidelines and technologies. Congress has not directed the creation of such an information sharing environment for the investigation of more traditional crimes in either the real or cyber worlds.

While there is not a sole clearinghouse for information sharing on traditional criminal investigations, there are a number of databases that contain a given subset of information. These include the FBI's Law Enforcement Online, Automated Fingerprint Identification System, National Crime Information Center, National Data Exchange, and Violent Criminal Apprehension Program; ATF's Arson & Explosives National Repository and Bomb Arson Tracking System; and the High Intensity Drug Trafficking Area Deconfliction, among others.[173] Through a 2006 nationwide survey, the Justice Statistics and Research Association (JSRA) identified 266 information sharing systems (that were either in place or under development) spanning 35 states and Canada.[174] These systems share information about crime at the national, regional, state, and county levels. Of these systems, 10% were identified as sharing national-level data. When survey respondents recommended system improvements, the most common suggestion involved including additional agencies in the information sharing system.[175]

Databases have been established to coordinate information on specific types of crime. For instance, the National Identity Crimes Law Enforcement (NICLE) was established to coordinate information on identity theft and related crimes.[176] This network, organized and led by the U.S. Attorney's Office for the Eastern District of Pennsylvania, consolidates information from local, state, and federal law enforcement agencies. Data in NICLE is available to nearly 100 law enforcement agencies through the Regional Information Sharing System Intranet (RISSNET).[177] The President's Identity Theft Task Force had recommended the establishment of a national database for law enforcement to consolidate information on identity theft.[178]

---

[172] For more information on the ISE, see CRS Report R40901, *Terrorism Information Sharing and the Nationwide Suspicious Activity Report Initiative: Background and Issues for Congress*, by Jerome P. Bjelopera. See also http://www.ise.gov/.

[173] For more databases, see the Justice Research and Statistics Association (JRSA), *Information Sharing Systems: A Survey of Law Enforcement*, July 31, 2006, p. 14, http://www.jrsa.org/pubs/reports/improving-crime-data/Info_Sharing.pdf.

[174] Ibid, p. 6. JSRA surveyed law enforcement analysts, Statistical Analysis Center directors, and Uniform Crime Reporting program managers.

[175] Ibid., p. 7.

[176] U.S. Department of Justice, United States Attorney, Eastern District of Pennsylvania, *Launch of the National Identity Crime Law Enforcement Network (NICLE)*, http://www.theiacp.org/investigateid/pdf/appendices/Launch-of-the-Natitonal-Identity-Crime-Law-Enforcement-Network-NICLE.pdf.

[177] The RISS program is funded and administered by DOJ's Bureau of Justice Assistance. For more information, see http://www.riss net/.

[178] The President's Identity Theft Task Force, *Combating Identity Theft: A Strategic Plan*, April 23, 2007, p. 56, http://www.identitytheft.gov/reports/StrategicPlan.pdf.

Public/Private Partnerships

Law enforcement has recognized the benefits of working with private entities in order to gather information and enhance investigations. One such partnership is InfraGard, through which the FBI gathers information on cybercrimes and other cases.[179] InfraGard is an FBI partnership with businesses, academic institutions, and other law enforcement agencies. Through this program, the Bureau can collect and disseminate information to private sector entities as well as other law enforcement partners. The InfraGard program began as a means to share cybercrime information, but its mission has expanded to include other crimes and threats, particularly those involving critical infrastructure.[180] As of November 2009, InfraGard had more than 33,000 members across 87 U.S. cities.[181]

Similar to InfraGard is the Domestic Security Alliance Council (DSAC).[182] DSAC is a security and intelligence-sharing initiative between the FBI, DHS, and the private sector, and the focus is on crimes impacting interstate commerce. These include computer intrusions, insider threats, fraud, theft of trade secrets, product tampering, and workplace violence. As of March 2011, DSAC had nearly 200 U.S. private sector companies and organizations.

Another partnership—the Law Enforcement Retail Partnership Network (LERPnet)—has been established to combat organized retail crime.[183] In 2006, through the Violence Against Women and Department of Justice Reauthorization Act of 2005,[184] Congress directed the Attorney General and the FBI to establish a clearinghouse within the private sector for information sharing between retailers and law enforcement. The result was LERPnet. It began as a partnership between the FBI, ICE, various local police departments, individual retailers, and retail organizations including the Food Marketing Institute (FMI), National Retail Federation (NRF), and Retail Industry Leaders Association (RILA). As of January 2010, LERPnet has been linked with the FBI's Law Enforcement Online (LEO) system, providing federal and local law enforcement with a direct link to retail industry crime reports.

Technology Implementation

Savvy criminals are constantly evolving their methods to stay paces ahead of law enforcement. They traverse through and around physical and cyber space, capitalizing on ever advancing technology to evade detection. In response, law enforcement has utilized an array of methods, from human intelligence to advanced technology to investigate these criminals.

---

[179] http://www.infragard net/index.php.

[180] Federal Bureau of Investigation, *InfraGard: A Parnership That Works*, March 8, 2010, http://www fbi.gov/news/stories/2010/march/infragard_030810.

[181] Statement of Steven R. Chabinsky, Deputy Assistant Director, Cyber Division, Federal Bureau of Investigation, before the U.S. Congress, Senate Committee on the Judiciary, Subcommittee on Terrorism and Homeland Security, *Cybersecurity: Preventing Terrorist Attacks and Protecting Privacy Rights in Cyberspace*, 111th Cong., 1st sess., November 17, 2009.

[182] Federal Bureau of Investigation, *Domestic Security: Combating Crime, Protecting Commerce*, March 14, 2011, http://www fbi.gov/news/stories/2011/march/security_031411.

[183] For more information on LERPnet, see http://www.lerpnet2.com/.

[184] P.L. 109-162, §1105, codified at 28 U.S.C. §509 note.

As discussed, Mexican drug traffickers have dug subterranean tunnels to smuggle illicit drugs from Mexico into the United States. The United States employs various tunnel detection technologies such as ground penetrating radar (GPR) to locate and shut down these tunnels.[185] GPR is limited, however, by factors such as soil condition and tunnel diameter and depth. Law enforcement may also use sonic equipment to detect the sounds of digging and tunnel construction as well as seismic technologies to detect blasts that may be indicative of tunnel excavation. U.S. officials have acknowledged that law enforcement currently does not have technology that is reliably able to detect the more sophisticated tunnels.[186] Rather, tunnels are more effectively discovered as a result of human intelligence and tips rather than technology. Indeed human intelligence, or HUMINT, "is the oldest method for collecting information, and until the technical revolution of the mid to late twentieth century, it was the primary source of intelligence. HUMINT is used mainly by the CIA [Central Intelligence Agency], the Department of State, the DoD [Department of Defense], and the FBI."[187] Further, the Interagency Threat Assessment and Coordination Group (ITACG) at the National Counterterrorism Center has indicated that "HUMINT can often collect information that is difficult or sometimes impossible to collect by other, more technical, means."[188]

As crime has transformed to involve more technology, law enforcement has moved to keep pace. Nonetheless, the FBI and others continue to recognize the value of human intelligence and confidential sources/informants. Reportedly, the FBI maintains over 15,000 such sources.[189] Even in cyber investigations, the FBI and other federal law enforcement agencies rely heavily on confidential sources. It has been estimated that "25% of hackers in the US may have been recruited by the federal authorities to be their eyes and ears."[190] Both the FBI and the USSS have had success in infiltrating the underground world of hackers, and hackers-turned-informants have worked not only with law enforcement, but with the military as well. For instance, in 2004 Adrian Lamo, a notorious hacker, pled guilty to hacking into *The New York Times*'s internal network containing personally identifiable information of *Times* contributors.[191] He also reportedly accessed the *Times*'s LexisNexis subscription account, creating fictitious usernames and conducting unauthorized searches. In 2010, Lamo was purportedly contacted by Bradley Manning, a U.S. Army intelligence analyst who is alleged to have passed classified cables to Wikileaks. After Manning supposedly claimed responsibility for the leaks, Lamo reportedly turned Manning over to the Army and FBI.[192]

Despite the use of human intelligence, advances in technology, outmoded laws, and a lack of resources, training, and personnel can keep law enforcement "in the dark" as criminals evade

---

[185] For more information, see http://www.geophysical.com/militarysecurity htm.

[186] Ken Stier, "Underground Threat: Tunnels Pose Trouble from Mexico to Middle East," *Time*, May 2, 2009.

[187] Office of the Director of National Intelligence, *How Do We Collect Intelligence?*, http://www.dni.gov/what_collection htm.

[188] National Counterterrorism Center, Interagency Threat Assessment and Coordination Group, *Intelligence Guide for First Responders*, p. 7, http://www nctc.gov/docs/itacg_guide_for_first_responders.pdf.

[189] Evan Ratliff, "The Mark; A Reporter at Large," *The New Yorker*, May 2, 2011, p. 56.

[190] Ed Pilkington, "One in four US hackers 'is an FBI informer'," *The Guardian*, June 6, 2011, http://www.guardian.co.uk/technology/2011/jun/06/us-hackers-fbi-informer.

[191] U.S. Department of Justice, "Hacker Pleads Guilty in Manhattan Federal Court to Illegally Accessing New York Times Computer Network ," press release, January 8, 2004, http://www.justice.gov/criminal/cybercrime/lamoPlea htm.

[192] Kevin Poulsen and Kim Zetter, "'I Can't Believe What I'm Confessing to You': The Wikileaks Chats," *Wired.com*, June 10, 2010, http://www.wired.com/threatlevel/2010/06/wikileaks-chat/.

detection.[193] Because of this very issue, the FBI has created the "Going Dark" initiative. This initiative is based on the premise that rapid changes in technology may impede the Bureau's ability to conduct electronic surveillance.[194] Law enforcement has indicated that while they have the legal authorities to do so, they may not have the technological capabilities.

Congress may debate how to best enable law enforcement to leverage their authorities and available technology to conduct necessary investigations while also protecting personal communications and privacy. One concern of privacy advocates is that enabling law enforcement to more easily obtain information from communications services providers could jeopardize individuals' privacy.[195] Some have suggested that "[a]lthough massive penetration into criminal communities may help curtail some unlawful activities, the invasive penetration into communities and the absolute control over whatever happens in the digital space amount to disruption of natural rights."[196] Policy makers may weigh whether the best means to aid federal law enforcement involve bolstering authorities to use encryption-breaking technologies, enhancing training of law enforcement personnel so they can best leverage existing authorities and technologies, or encouraging agencies to direct their manpower and financial resources to investigating cybercrimes, among other options.

Conclusion

The operational realities of 21st century crime and policing present significant challenges to U.S. policy makers. In particular, the interplay between borders, criminal turf, cyberspace, and law enforcement jurisdiction is such that policies directed toward countering crime in one reality will impact crime and law enforcement countermeasures in other realities. As such, Congress may choose to debate a host of legislative and oversight options to most effectively empower law enforcement.

Legislatively, Congress may consider whether law enforcement has the existing authorities, technology, and resources—both monetary and manpower—to counter 21st century criminals. For instance, given that many crimes are increasingly trans-border in nature, Congress may deliberate whether certain offenses are best criminalized at the state or federal level. If Congress determines that these crimes may be most effectively countered at the federal level, policy makers may consider expanding federal law enforcement's statutory authorities to investigate these offenses. Policy makers may also consider whether to direct existing or additional resources toward bolstering federal law enforcement agents' skills and abilities to counter modern day threats. For example, Congress may direct the allocation of agent resources toward combating more

---

[193] See Freedom of Information Act (FOIA) documents provided by the FBI to the Electronic Frontier Foundation (EFF), p. 120, http://www.eff.org/files/20110207_FBI_Going_Dark_Release_Part_4.pdf. Links to the all relevant FOIA documents provided to the EFF are referenced by Jennifer Lynch, "Newly Released Documents Detail FBI's Plan to Expand Federal Surveillance Laws," *Electronic Frontier Foundation*, February 15, 2011, http://www.eff.org/deeplinks/2011/02/newly-released-documents-detail-fbi-s-plan-expand.

[194] See Freedom of Information Act (FOIA) documents provided by the FBI to the Electronic Frontier Foundation (EFF), p. 110, http://www.eff.org/files/20110207_FBI_Going_Dark_Release_Part_4.pdf.

[195] Declan McCullagh, "FBI to Announce New Net-Wiretapping Push," *PrivacyInc*, February 16, 2011, http://news.cnet.com/8301-31921_3-20032518-281 html.

[196] Jijo Jacob, "FBI moles run illegal sites that deal in hackers' loot of sensitive data," *International Business Times*, June 7, 2011, http://www.ibtimes.com/articles/158620/20110607/fbi-hacking-hackers-hacktivists-moles-sites-lulz-security-lulzsec-sony-infragard-one-in-four-anonymo htm.

traditional, yet evolving, crimes such as financial fraud. Policy makers may also choose to direct law enforcement training to enhance agents' technological savvy such that policing efforts can keep pace with modern-day criminals. Further, state and local law enforcement agencies are also tasked with countering these criminal threats. As such, Congress may debate whether to provide financial, technological, or investigative support to state and local law enforcement operations.

In exercising its oversight responsibilities, Congress may examine whether law enforcement is utilizing existing mechanisms to effectively coordinate investigations and share information. U.S. law enforcement has, particularly since the terrorist attacks of September 11, 2001, increasingly relied on intelligence-led policing, enhanced interagency cooperation (through formal and informal interagency agreements as well as fusion centers and task forces), and technological implementation to confront 21st century crime. Nonetheless, there have been notable impediments in implementing effective information sharing systems and relying on up-to-date technology. As such, policy makers may consider what is the appropriate level of interagency information sharing and whether law enforcement is effectively achieving this goal. Congress may also wish to explore whether existing inter-agency agreements are being adequately formulated, implemented, and overseen by the relevant agencies.

Author Contact Information

Kristin M. Finklea
Specialist in Domestic Security
kfinklea@crs.loc.gov, 7-6259

www.ingramcontent.com/pod-product-compliance
Lightning Source LLC
Chambersburg PA
CBHW081404170526
45166CB00010B/3197